To my most favorite photog,

You beautifully documented these past four years, so I hope this book now inspires you to do fun things with them! I will miss all of our baking cabinet self-timer pics, but now you'll have the amazing city of Chicago as your backdrop. Never stop snapping pics!

Love,

Lis

► PHOTOCRAFT

Cool Things to Do with the Pictures You Love

PHOTOCRAFT

Caroline Herter | Laurie Frankel | Laura Lovett

BULFINCH PRESS
New York • Boston • London

BULFINCH PRESS

Hachette Book Group USA

237 Park Avenue, New York, NY 10017

Visit our Web site at www.bulfinchpress.com

First Edition: September 2005

Updated Edition: April 2007

ISBN: 978-0-8212-6195-8

     0-8212-6195-9

Library of Congress Control Number 2005924278

Published by arrangement with

HERTER STUDIO LLC

432 Elizabeth Street

San Francisco, CA 94114

Designed by Laura Lovett

Printed in Singapore

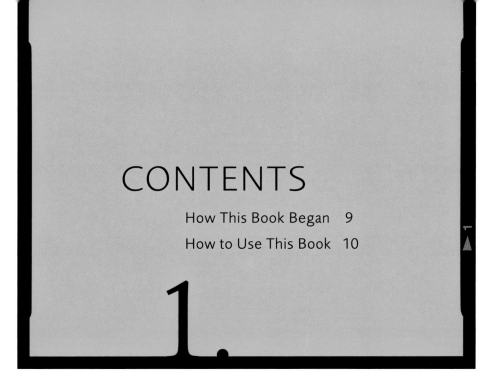

CONTENTS

1.

PHOTOCRAFT 101 13

PHOTO PLAY

Learn While You Create 47

2.

EXPANDING YOUR REPERTOIRE

Take It to the Next Level 95

3.

HOW THIS BOOK BEGAN

Several years ago I happened on an extraordinary collection of family albums dating back to the late 1800s. Meticulously kept (in the days when one actually had that sort of time) by my grandmother and her mother before her, they were filled with images that not only linked me to my past, but were also exceptional photographically—like this gorgeous picture of my grandmother "Mac," looking like she had stepped right out of a Ralph Lauren ad.

I persuaded my family to let me take the albums home to California, where I set about trying to repair and preserve them for future generations. In the process, I became a little obsessed; there were so many amazing pictures! I just couldn't imagine having to haul out the albums every time I wanted to look at them, much less share them with an extended family of sixty!

So I started to play around. I photographed a few of my favorite images with slide film (no affordable digital cameras then) and took them to a professional photo lab to have them cleaned up, enlarged, and beautifully printed as though they were fine art originals. Framed and hung on my living room walls, they created an elegant and personally meaningful gallery of artwork at a fraction of the cost of "real" photographs. I was so excited about how they looked that I framed duplicates as holiday gifts for my family that year—the first in a series of fledgling experiments that grew into the idea for this book.

I am not inherently a crafty person, though I have a pretty good eye and use it in my work. But basically, I have no patience, no knowledge, no skills, and no time. I have a PC and a three-year-old inkjet printer, copier, fax, and flatbed scanner (one of those very affordable all-in-one machines, which I highly recommend). When this book began, I knew nothing about materials, scanning, or digital image manipulation. I didn't know what a service bureau or a solvent was. And I didn't own a digital camera. What I did have was a lot of great pictures and some wacky ideas for turning them into cool and crafty things that would dress up my house and make easy and affordable gifts for the people I love.

Toward that end, I formed a team with Laura Lovett, the book's designer and project manager, and Laurie Frankel, our brilliant photographer—both of whom have great ideas, great taste, and quite a few more skills than I do. With a few credited exceptions, the ideas in this book are ours, and for better or worse, all of the projects actually have been made by us. This was deliberate. We wanted to experience what you will—the joy of making these things ourselves, learning as we went, and coming to love the unexpected result, which, more often than not, was far better than anything we could have imagined.

By its very nature, "photocraft" is an intensely personal craft. Perfection is not the goal, and there is no right or wrong result. When you add your own very special pictures to the mix, "home-made" becomes "heart-made" at its very best.

—Caroline Herter

HOW TO USE THIS BOOK

The best way to get the most out of *Photocraft* is to use the book in order. Each section ("Photocraft 101," "Photo Play," and "Expanding Your Repertoire") provides the knowledge, skills, and hands-on experience you need to move on to the next. This is not to say you can't sneak an attempt at one of the tougher projects without practicing on an easy one first, or that you can't muddle your way through without ever reading "Photocraft 101," but we can guarantee that unless you're already a pro, you'll have an easier time and make much better projects if you take it one section, one step, at a time.

• *Read "Photocraft 101"*
Even if you ignore all of our other suggestions, please read this section through from beginning to end. All of the concepts, tools, terms, techniques, and materials needed to make the projects are explained here, along with recommended brands, valuable tips, and important safety ⚠ and copyright information. You'll find the Photocraft Pantry at the end of the section, along with metric conversions if you need them. No matter what your level, it's a terrific orientation, jam-packed with helpful and interesting information that will get your creative juices going, boost your confidence, and better your results.

• *Armchair Shop*
Browse the Resources section at the back of the book. Use this and your local phone book to become familiar with online and local suppliers, so you know where to find what you need when the time comes. If you're feeling brave, pay a visit to your nearest copy shop, camera shop, and service bureau to see what services they provide. And if you're ready to commit, stock up on some basic supplies from the Photocraft Pantry.

• *Learn While You Create*
Some of the coolest ideas in the book are also the easiest. The projects in "Photo Play" have been designed to teach (and let you experiment with) the techniques and materials you'll need to complete the more advanced projects later on. You'll learn about software tricks (Your Own Andy Warhol, page 84), printing on specialty papers (Festive Votives, page 59), ironing transfers onto fabric (Photo Transfers, page 48) and ceramic tile (Tile Coasters, page 60), laminating (Pet Place Mats, page 81), stickering (The Coolest Tissue Box, page 50), and simple paper fabrication (Note Cards, page 70), to name just a few.

• *Take It to the Next Level*
In "Expanding Your Repertoire," you'll move on to a whole new batch of slightly more ambitious projects that build on what you've learned. Make a decorative pillow (Throw Pillow, page 113), a gorgeous Japanese screen (Folding Screen, page 145), a hanging "mural" (Carla's Hanging Mural, page

142), a baby quilt (Antique Shoes Baby Quilt, page 115), a side table (Tile-Topped Plant Stand, page 134), lampshades (Vellum Lampshades, page 139), and more.

• *Invent Your Own*

What if you printed extra negative-strip stickers from The Coolest Tissue Box project and used them as fridge magnets, or applied the silk-printing and quilting techniques to a duvet cover instead? This is the true joy of photocraft. The possibilities are endless, and if we've done our job well, you'll have all the tools, techniques, and inspiration you need to create a photocraft collection of your very own. Digital images are the starting point of many of the projects. We know that the whole idea of image editing will be scary to many of you at first, but trust us—ten minutes of playing around and you'll be totally hooked. Before you know it, you'll be making magic! You'll also begin to understand one of the great things about photocraft—that your worst "mistakes" often become your best creations.

HOW TO READ A PROJECT "RECIPE"

There are 42 photocraft projects in the book. Some of them are what we call "Snapshots," quick and easy one-page ideas that require no more than a paragraph to explain. The rest follow a classic recipe format, with tools and materials substituting for ingredients. You'll find step-by-step instructions, tips, variations, and helpful illustrations throughout.

There are four "ingredient" categories in the projects: Images, Computer Tools, Pantry Checklist, and Materials. All are easily cross-referenced to similar headings in "Photocraft 101" should you need a quick refresher course about any of them.

Images We note the quantity, size, type (digital or prints) and resolution requirements, if there are any. Resolution is a key factor in digital image quality. See page 18 for more information.

Computer Tools / Software Because there are so many different programs with different terminology and features, we had to decide on a standard for this book. We chose ADOBE PHOTOSHOP ELEMENTS 4.0, which was used to create all of the projects that require image-editing work and is the reference for the terminology used throughout. We recommend it, not only because it will make following project instructions exponentially easier but because, as of this writing, it is by far the best basic image-editing program out there. It's easy to learn, fun to play with, versatile enough for all of the projects in the book (and more), and readily available for under $80.00. Unless you're already using "grown-up" PHOTOSHOP, we strongly recommend you download a free 30-day trial from www.adobe.com. This will give you plenty of time to learn the program, play around, even try it out on one of the projects before you make up your mind.

NOTE: Even if you decide to stick with the software you've got, you'll need to compare the names of ELEMENTS commands to those used in your program so you know how to translate unfamiliar terminology. Keep in mind that ELEMENTS 4.0 has many more features than most of the image-editing software programs bundled with digital cameras, scanners, and printers; you may not be able to find an equivalent function in every case.

Computer Tools / Hardware We list the hardware (inkjet or laser printer or photocopier) needed to complete the project. If you don't have it or can't do it, don't worry; "Photocraft 101" tells you how and where to outsource virtually anything.

Pantry Checklist These are the project "ingredients" that may already be in your pantry and that you'll likely use in other projects (in other words, don't worry about overbuying if only large sizes are available). You'll find the full Photocraft Pantry on page 44. All of these items are available from craft and art supply stores, Web sites, one of our recommended resources, or tracked down in your local phone book.

Materials What you will need to buy specifically for the project. You can always "Google" any product to locate a source, but we have also provided contact information in the resource section for the more esoteric items, as well as for materials—from specialty papers and printable silks to transparent adhesives and waterproof sealants. We list brand names when they are either markedly better than the competition or are the only option available. All of the basic photo and craft materials you'll encounter in the book are thoroughly explained in "Photocraft 101," with our recommendations and tips for how to choose, what to expect, and how to get the best result from each.

1. PHOTOCRAFT 101

THOSE OF YOU WHO CAN CLAIM BOTH DIGITAL AND CRAFT PROFICIENCY, BY ALL MEANS, DIVE RIGHT INTO THE PROJECTS. FOR THE REST, NO MATTER HOW EXPERIENCED IN EITHER AREA, READ ON: THERE'S SOMETHING IN THIS SECTION YOU NEED TO KNOW. You may find it in Your Images (selecting, sourcing, shooting, permissions, preserving, storing), The Digital World (digitizing, editing, hardware, software, outsourcing), The Material World (papers, inks, adhesives, solvents, sealants, archival options, framing), or all three—you won't know until you get there. And even if you think you already know it, skim it, don't skip it; there are terrific tips throughout for photocrafters of all skill levels.

In "Photocraft 101," we share our learn-by-doing know-how. But even more, this key section reflects the expertise of immensely talented and knowledgeable artist-photographers and crafts professionals, our consultants for the projects and techniques that appear in this book. As you read it through, please keep in mind that we have set a very high standard for quality, so beginners and intermediates have something to aspire to and experienced crafters and digital artists can learn something, too. That said, Caroline got through the projects she made for this book with no image-editing skills at all. Her projects were done on an old inkjet all-in-one printer, using the copier function to enlarge, reduce, and print. She didn't really know how to use her digital camera (though she took some great shots by accident!), and she had no idea what the resolution was for any of the images she used, but she now knows why some of them looked awful no matter what she did. Her grandmother's albums, which she treasures, have not been stored in archival boxes until very recently, and she flipped them onto her scanner with impunity. They survived. This is not to say you should be so cavalier, but it is to urge you not to worry overmuch about getting it "right." "Right" in photocraft-land means only one thing: that you like the way your project looks.

YOUR IMAGES

FINDING THE RIGHT IMAGES is the first and most important step no matter which project they will be used for. When in doubt, look for images that are simple, graphic, colorful, sharp, and have strong contrast (darks and lights). These will be clearer both enlarged and reduced and will hold up better when transferred.

Many of your favorite images will doubtless be pictures from your own life and that of your family, from the yellow-tinted pictures in your grandparents' albums to the images that are on your digital camera right now. Sift through that old shoebox, album, or what we like to call our "digital dumpsite" (all the thousands of images downloaded from our digital cameras). Dozens of funny, touching, and beautiful images will jump out at you.

Sourcing

Your boxes of snapshots are only one source of imagery. The projects in this book use all kinds of pictures, culled from many different places. We encourage you to think broadly as you create an image collection. Besides photos of family, friends, and vacation highlights, gather other kinds of pictures that speak to you—landscapes, still lifes, interiors, pictures of buildings, gardens, strangers wearing strange hats, abstract images. They will all have uses in projects in this book. Find them at friends' houses, flea markets, book shops, and junk and antique stores.

The Internet is also a great resource, particularly if you have specific themes in mind. A Google image search will instantly provide you with a wealth of choices on a million different subjects (try it—type in keywords such as "driftwood," "baby carriage," or "sheep"). There are also many companies on the Internet that sell or rent images for general use. Check out www.istockphoto.com for its reasonable prices, but there are many others as well (do a search for "stock photos" or "clip art").

Shooting

And don't forget about taking your own photographs. Once you get going, you'll start to view the world around you differently—you'll see picture-worthy abstract compositions, incredible colors, panoramic views, funky shop signs, worn lettering, and so on. Sometimes you'll get an image in your head (like the blueberries in Your Own Brand, page 75) and you'll have to create it yourself (in this case, by throwing a couple of blueberries on the kitchen counter as Caroline did). The best part about using your own pictures is that you never need to worry about getting the photographer's permission to use them, though you do need to worry about whether your subject will be happy!

Frish collects fine art photography and "found" photographs, which are among her favorites. Gathered at flea markets and antique stores, and occasionally purchased from dealers, the images on her dining room wall all feature subjects who are flying, diving, leaping, or stepping off into thin air.

Be aware of the following when downloading images from the Internet: First, many images that you can download for free are both small and low resolution, rendering them unsuitable for some of the projects in this book. More important, you must be careful not to misuse copyrighted images or to invade someone's privacy. In general, the rules are:

• If you didn't shoot it yourself, or don't know for certain that it's free to use, get a signed permissions letter from the photographer.

• If you don't know for certain that the subject(s) will be happy to have their face on your lamp, get a signed model release.

• If your "subject" is someone else's creation (fabric design, a street mural, a famous contemporary building, an ad, a book cover, a brand), get a signed permissions letter from the creator. (In other words, don't photograph an Armani pattern for your scarf!)

• If you find yourself thinking about selling your photocraft wares to the public, you must be absolutely rigorous about getting legally airtight, written permissions from your photographers and subjects. Ask an intellectual property attorney to adapt a standard permissions letter and model release to your needs; the money you spend now for peace of mind will be far less than what you might have to spend down the road for a settlement.

Organizing

If you have a well-organized image collection, finding the right pictures for a new project needn't be an all-day affair. Here are some ways to streamline the process: Mark your old albums with Post-it notes or, better yet, if you have a digital camera, rephotograph your favorite shots and transfer them to your computer. Pull your favorite loose photos together in a special "photocraft" box. Create a new folder on your computer named "Photocraft" and put your choicest images into it, grouping them thematically for easy access later on. The point is to create one or two places where you can instantly retrieve the pictures you love most.

Preserving

Traditional and digital prints raise different preservation, or archival, issues. Digital images should be safely backed up (see Storage Options, page 20). If you are altering an image, be sure to work on a copy and save your original. Once you change and save it, there is no going back.

Prints, on the other hand, are much more vulnerable. If you want digital prints (either outsourced or your own) to outlast you, be sure to use archival papers and inks (there are lots to choose from; see Resources, page 152). But don't count on photo or laser copies making it to the next century; for now at least, there is no such thing as archival toner.

Most important, your existing photos (everything from precious family photos to flea market finds to fine art prints) are subject to fading and deterioration if they are not stored properly—away from critters that could nibble at the edges, moisture, excessive heat, dirt and dust, and, especially, light. Consider these suggestions for the best possible (professional-level) care of your prints:

Light Avoid exposing your photos to direct sunlight and fluorescent light, which will both cause your photos to fade prematurely. Store loose photos in archival boxes and albums (see Storing, below). When deciding where to hang framed photographs, consider the amount of light they will receive throughout the day (the less the better) and protect them under UV-resistant sheet acrylic plastic like Plexiglas (available at any frame shop). If the perfect spot is on a wall or table that gets direct sunlight, frame a copy and store the original in a safe place.

Temperature and humidity The ideal temperature for photo storage is 68 degrees with 30% to 40% relative humidity. If you don't have access to a temperature-controlled room or closet, think about storing your photos where you'd be comfortable sitting year after year. Attics, garages, and basements are not good choices—they tend to have more temperature fluctuations and humidity extremes than the rest of the house.

Environmental hazards Keep your precious photos away from fumes and air pollutants. Wait at least a month before leaving them in a room that's been freshly painted with oil paint, and don't store them in closets with cleaning supplies.

Handling The less you handle your photos, the less likelihood of tearing, creasing, or crumpling them. Always hold photographs by the edges, keeping your fingers off the image. When you do sift through them, it's best to wear light cotton gloves to protect the images from the oils in your skin.

Storing
Store large numbers of photos layered between sheets of 100% cotton bond acid-free paper in metal or acid-free cardboard boxes, or in archival plastic sheets. Avoid glue, tape, staples, rubber bands, and paper clips, which can cause stains, scratches, and dents. Beware of all wood and wood products (including paper) unless they are labeled acid-free.

One of the most common mistakes is to store irreplaceable photographs in cheap photo albums (albums with adhesive pages are always a no-no). Buy albums made of high-quality, archival materials and use photo corners, just the way your grandmother did. Store albums handed down from previous generations in archival boxes.

THE DIGITAL WORLD

IN AN IDEAL WORLD, YOUR ENTIRE IMAGE COLLECTION WOULD BE DIGITIZED to preserve your original prints, slides, and negatives, which should never be used in projects. But unless you have way more time than we do, it's more likely that the images you choose will be a mix of traditional prints (like the best picks from your great-grandmother's album, old postcards from the flea market, and more) and digital images downloaded from the Internet, sent to you by e-mail, or taken with your digital camera.

In traditional film-based photography, the camera records the image on film, which is then chemically processed in a darkroom and printed on sensitized photo paper. Images taken with a digital camera, on the other hand, are captured electronically and can be transferred directly to your home computer for easy access, organization, storage, enhancement, editing, and printing on a remarkably broad range of papers and fabrics. For all these reasons, digital images are the preferred starting point for most photocraft projects.

On the other hand, if you already own a film-based camera, you don't need to feel pressured to go digital just yet. You can easily convert your original prints to digital format by scanning them, either on your own scanner or at a local photo store or service bureau where they will be scanned onto a photo CD. Even a moderately priced scanner will yield great results. And once an image is scanned, you can alter and print it just as you would an image from your digital camera. If you aren't ready to invest in digital equipment, you can use photocopies instead in many projects.

► DIGITAL IMAGE QUALITY: It's All About Resolution

If the images on your screen—or more likely, the images from your printer—are not as sharp as they could be, if the edges seem jagged and the pixels are showing, or the contrast is less than ideal, chances are it's a problem of resolution. Resolution affects every step of digital image-making, whether you are snapping a picture with a digital camera, scanning it, or printing it in final form. Once you "get" this critical concept, you'll be better able to create images that look good to you and to troubleshoot those that don't.

Briefly, resolution is the total amount of information your computer has about a specific digital image. There are two types of resolution: *image resolution*, which is determined when you shoot or scan your pictures, and *printer resolution*, which can be adjusted when you print. To get the best prints possible from your equipment, you must pay attention to the resolution at both of these stages. No amount of printer-resolution tweaking will compensate for an image that was shot or scanned at too low a resolution.

IMAGE RESOLUTION

If you examine a digital image through a magnifying glass, you'll see tiny, colored squares—pixels (see examples at right). Resolution refers to how many pixels there are in one square inch of image, and can be expressed either as dpi (dots per inch) or ppi (pixels per inch)—both mean the same thing. The fewer the pixels per inch (the lower the resolution), the more your eye will register individual pixels and the more angular or "pixilated" your image will appear. Conversely, the more pixels per inch (the higher the resolution), the harder they are to see, and the more seamless your result.

If your image has 300 dots in every inch of its final printed size, which is what we recommend, pixels are invisible, yielding digital prints that are as beautiful as their traditional film-based counterparts. At this resolution, you will have many more options when adjusting and printing your images, particularly when they are enlarged. Think of it this way: Your original digital image has a fixed number of pixels. When you blow up that image, that same pixel count is spread over a much larger area. The rule: The more pixels you start with, the more you can enlarge the image before the pixels become visible. Even a one-inch-square postage stamp scanned at 300 dpi won't work as a poster (just imagine how far apart those 300 little pixels would be from each other in a 24- x 36-inch print!). Should you get hooked on digital imaging, however, and start producing large-scale fine art prints, you will want to print at a resolution of no less than 720 dpi in order to get clarity of detail and good tonal range at large sizes.

If your image was shot or scanned too small or at too low a resolution, all is not lost. Most image-editing software offer a handy feature called resampling. Use it to add pixels if you want to enlarge an image or delete pixels to shrink it. Keep in mind, though, that resampling does affect picture quality; do your own tests to see how much you can resample before your image noticeably deteriorates. The rule in commercial printing is to rescan rather than resample if you enlarge an image by 30% or more. This is a good rule to follow at home, too.

▶ **TIP** Here's an irritating fact of digital life: An image may look great on your computer screen, but be jagged and rough when printed. Why? Because computer monitors can't display anything more than 72 dpi (dots per inch). That means an image that is 80 dpi and one that is 600 dpi may look identical on your monitor. However, even the lowliest printer can print 300 dpi or more, so those missing pixels will be obvious once you print. To prevent disappointment, make it a habit to check the size of your file and its image resolution before you print (IMAGE/RESIZE/ IMAGE SIZE).

Digital photograph, 72 dpi x 300%

Digital photograph, 300 dpi x 300%

PRINTER RESOLUTION

If 300 dpi is the ideal image resolution, why do printers have settings of 600, 720, and even 1440 dpi? That's because image and printer resolutions are not the same. Printer resolution refers to the way printers deposit ink on paper. Inkjet printers have nozzles that release tiny droplets of ink, with resolutions that range from 300 to 1440 dpi (a reference to the number of nozzles and the number of colors each nozzle lays down). Most desktop laser printers, which print with heat-set powdered toner, have a resolution of 600 dpi. A printer resolution of 720 dpi is considered ideal photo quality.

Printing software varies widely, but if you explore the options available in your PRINT dialog box, you will figure out how to specify resolution, or at least choose between DRAFT (FAST), NORMAL, and BEST quality. Selecting a higher (BEST or QUALITY) print resolution will produce better results, but will slow down your printer and eat up more ink (a hidden cost that can add up quickly). On a low-end printer, BEST quality is definitely worth the trade-off in time and ink. On the other hand, the DRAFT setting will print quickly and use less ink, producing an acceptable print in many cases. Experiment. As with everything in photocraft, your eye decides; if you like what you see, go with it!

▶ HARDWARE & SOFTWARE

The digital revolution that freed photographers from the darkroom gave them a new creative tool kit: digital cameras, powerful computers, and amazing software, as well as sophisticated printers, versatile scanners, even photocopiers from the local copy shop. This new technology is so simple that all of us can produce spectacular images anywhere we can access a computer. The dining room or home office is the new photo lab. Be sure your current computer has enough memory to run an image-editing program and handle image files. Working with digital images requires lots and lots of RAM (random access memory), so install as much as you can afford, with a minimum of 512 megabytes. You can never have too much!

STORAGE OPTIONS

Collecting digital images on your computer and saving them in multiple versions can quickly eat up the available space on your hard drive. Weekly or monthly (depending on how fast and furiously you're collecting images), save your files onto another media. You'll both protect your images and keep your computer running lean and mean. These storage tools are the best available right now.

CDs and DVDs As one CD holds up to 700 megabytes worth of data, CDs are currently a fast and inexpensive way to store lots of images. DVDs can store even more (4.7 gigabytes). Most new computers have a CD or DVD burner built in (you can also buy one as a separate component).

External hard drive/flash drive Plug an external hard drive into your computer, then unplug it when you're done to store in a safe place between backups. These drives are available in a range of storage sizes and are a safe, easy, and convenient backup option. Even cheaper are the new mini flash drives that can hold as much as 4 gigabytes.

DIGITAL CAMERAS

See it. Shoot it. E-mail it. Print it. Digital cameras are all about instant gratification. No more trudging to the drugstore and the endless waiting until your prints come back to see if you like (or hate) them. With a digital camera you can see your shot that moment, delete a failure and immediately reshoot, load the image on your computer, and zip it to everyone you know—all within a matter of minutes. Who wouldn't be smitten with such amazing and amazingly easy technology? There are so many cameras and options to choose from. Here's what to look for when buying a digital camera.

Batteries Given the high power consumption of digital cameras, make sure that your camera's batteries are rechargeable. This holds true regardless of whether it takes standard AA batteries or the more high-priced, but powerful lithium-ion batteries, sold in proprietary formats specific for each brand of camera. If offered a choice of AA batteries, the most long-lasting are lithium, followed by MiMH (Nickel Metal Hydride); least preferable are standard Nickel Cadmium batteries. You can drain your camera's batteries in many ways, but the most voracious abuser of battery life is a display screen left on continuously (shut it off if your battery is running low).

Controls Choose from basic point-and-shoot to features for action photos, close-ups, and shooting at night. Multiple options give you more ways to control quality. On the other hand, do you really need that many extra bells and whistles? Be honest with yourself. Will you take the time to learn how to use them? Do you want to have to consider them each time you take a picture?

Megapixels How many? That is the big question. The quality of a digital image is determined by the number of the sensors in the camera's chip, which is described in megapixels. More megapixels mean better image quality and more options for editing and printing. More megapixels also mean higher cost. Most amateur photographers will get great results with a 7- (or less) megapixel camera. But technology and prices change so fast that a just-released 10-megapixel model might cost the same as the 7-megapixel model it replaced. Check prices and options before you buy.

Memory cards/Storage cards A memory card serves the same function in a digital camera as film does in a conventional camera—a removable device that captures the images taken. Unlike film, a memory card can be erased and reused, a feature that somewhat justifies its hefty price (although prices continue to drop, so the cost per megabyte or gigabyte is dropping, too). The more megabytes a card has, the more images it will hold. Currently, you'll have to choose among a number of memory-card formats; one format doesn't work for all digital cameras and card readers. If you are buying a new digital camera, be sure to see how easy it is to find the card format your camera requires.

Zoom The actual movement of the camera's lens to make an image appear closer is optical zoom. (Ignore a camera's digital zoom—it's of very little use and is a feature that should be turned off.) Most digital cameras have at least 3x optical zoom, and some of the more expensive models may have a 4x, 5x, or even 10x optical zoom. Choose the zoom that fits your needs and budget.

Choose your format Shoot using RAW setting if available, which records the most information but also consumes the biggest chunk of your memory card. Many digital cameras shoot only in JPEG file format. You can achieve great results with JPEGs, but they are compressed files, which means that select pixels are removed in order to create smaller file sizes. After a certain point of enlargement the image will start to look poor, so they are not a good choice for large blow-ups. You'll want to save your images in TIFF file format when you transfer them to your computer.

Choose your image settings These are camera features (their names can vary from brand to brand) that let you set the resolution and file size of your photographs. For example, *Compression settings* (often labeled as NORMAL, FINE, and SUPERFINE) gives you a choice as to how much compression is applied to the file (see Choose your format, above). *Resolution settings* has to do with the size of the image you take. A setting of SMALL will produce images small enough to be sent over the Internet, MEDIUM will give you a good 4- x 6-inch print, and LARGE will capture an image that can be printed 8 x 10 inches and larger. If you select LARGE with SUPERFINE compression, you will be able to fit the least number of photographs on each memory card but they will be the highest quality possible.

Turn off the Unsharp Mask filter This filter increases contrast in your image to make it appear sharper. It is better to apply this filter later with your image-editing software.

Adjust your ISO settings These control the camera sensor's sensitivity to light. Traditionally, you want a lower ISO setting in bright light and a higher one in dim light. If your camera lets you select different ISO settings, try to use the lowest setting possible for a particular lighting situation. Similar to film speed on traditional cameras, the higher the number, the grainier the images will look when enlarged. A lower setting such as ISO 100 will give you sharper enlargements than a setting of 400.

Learn how to use the White Balance setting Familiarity with this feature, which interprets the color temperature of the light, will enable you to take digital photos that are the right colors, free of unsightly and difficult-to-remove color casts.

SCANNERS

We'll say it again: You don't need a digital camera to create digitized images! Scanners convert printed pictures into digital files that can be stored in your computer, ready to play with and print. Scanners can digitize anything: family snapshots, vintage albums, postcards, pages from a favorite album or book—anything that fits on the glass bed of the scanner. And if you mess up, you can always rescan, a real convenience.

There are two types of scanners for home use: *Film scanners* scan from negatives or slides, and are the more expensive and of higher quality. *Flatbed scanners* are used to scan prints and other paper-based objects, although many have adapters for negatives and slides as well. Prices for scanners have

Easily made, high-quality scanned copies let you display cherished family photos free of worry that they will deteriorate. With the originals safely stored away, you can still have them out where they can be enjoyed, even in a sunny room where they would otherwise fade.

plummeted (like most computer hardware). If you have a film-based camera that you love to use, or work with lots of prints or negatives, you may want to consider buying a scanner rather than using a service bureau to digitize your images (a costly and time-consuming option). Here are the features that matter when buying a scanner.

Bit depth Scanner quality is determined by the number of colors—called bit depth or color depth—that a scanner can detect in your artwork. With digital pictures, as with painting, more lifelike images are possible only with a large palette of colors. Usually this means 16.7 million different colors (or 24-bit). Some scanners offer more bit depth, but 24-bit is as much as you need—most software and printers can't process anything more than that.

Computer interface The transfer of large amounts of picture data from scanner to computer can be slow, so you want to use the fastest connection possible. USB 2.0 connections are speediest: those working on Macs also have the option of FireWire connections. Know what connections your computer is compatible with, then buy a scanner that works with the fastest cables your computer allows.

Dynamic range How well a scanner detects detail in the shadows and highlights of your original photograph is its dynamic range. A good scanner should have a dynamic range of 3.6 or better.

Resolution Just as with all things digital, the quality of your image and the flexibility you have in working with it is dependent on its resolution. The resolution of flatbed scanners is typically described by the number of dots per inch (dpi), expressed in width times length, for example, 1200 x 2400 dpi. The higher the numbers, the better quality scanner you've got.

⬤ ⬤ ⬤ ⬤ ⬤ ⬤ ⬤ ▶ ACHIEVING GREAT RESULTS WITH YOUR SCANNER

To obtain a good scan, above all, get to know the software provided with your machine. Most scanner hardware in any one price range is pretty much equal, but the software can make a marked difference. Beyond that, here are a few handy tips that deliver great results.

Make a preview scan This allows your scanning software to determine the correct exposure, and enables you to crop if needed. Try to fit your MARQUEE selection tightly around your original. This helps reduce the size of your scan and will result in a more accurate exposure.

Turn off filters Turn off any sharpening, dust, scratch, or descreening filters in your scanning software. It is better to scan with all filters and presets turned off and make these adjustments with your image-editing software.

"Garbage in, garbage out" Remember that scanners only record what you give them. If you scan from a print processed at a 1-hour photo shop, where sensitive printing is not the norm, expect a similar result from your scanned image. Keep in mind that you'll get better scans—with greater detail and

higher print quality—from larger originals, as they provide the scanner with more information. Scanning from a negative rather than a print made from that negative also produces better results.

Choose final image size carefully The final image size will be determined by how high you set the scan resolution. If you haven't determined the size yet, make the scan larger than you think you'll need. You can always scale down if you have to.

PRINTERS

Printing your images has become simple, affordable, and permanent thanks to a wide range of new and extremely sophisticated color printers. More important, digital printing allows photographers great creativity and control. No more reliance on shiny sensitized photographic paper. Now you can print on gorgeous craft papers, watercolor paper, artist's canvas, and even fabric, all with strikingly different results. Widely available now are "photo printers" that do not need a computer to operate, as they let you print directly from your digital camera or memory card. Currently their adjustment capabilities are usually limited to sizing and cropping, and many only print a 4- x 6-inch size. However, as with all things digital, this is changing rapidly.

Two types of printers are commonly available: *inkjet*, which puts down droplets of liquid ink, and *color laser*, which puts down powdered toner that is set with heat.

INKJET PRINTERS

You can make stunning prints with even the least expensive inkjet printer. If you haven't used one for a while, you'll be amazed at how much they've improved and how many there are to choose from. All offer excellent print quality at modest prices, and print on a wide range of media. If you have an all-in-one office machine that copies, prints, scans, and faxes, it uses inkjet technology, and all of the following discussion applies.

Inkjet printers are slower than laser printers if you need multiple copies, and they can run through the ink supply fairly quickly. Replacement ink cartridges tend to be expensive, and higher quality inkjet papers can also bite into your budget. But the results are worth it.

Be sure to have your printer cleaned and serviced once a year. Regular maintenance will extend its life and improve the quality of your prints. Most local computer stores and repair centers offer this service. Between servicing, keep printer mechanisms pristine by using a can of compressed air to blow away dust and lint.

Once you outgrow the capabilities of your little tabletop inkjet printer, you may want to consider a large-format inkjet printer. Epson, Hewlett Packard, and Canon all make high-end printers with eight to twelve color cartridges that yield a much greater depth and range of color tones, and carry a comparatively higher price tag, of course. These printers can accomplish all the usual printing tasks, as well as print in wide widths and on roll stock, and your photographs will look stunning.

Keep these features in mind when shopping for an inkjet printer. But above all, trust your eyes. The best way to choose a printer is to review images printed by the models you are considering. A printer with tons of features is no compensation if you don't like the look of the finished prints. Computer and electronic trade shows are a great place to comparison shop.

Borderless capabilities If printing edge-to-edge (also called "full bleed") appeals to you then include this feature when buying your printer.

Number of ink colors A printer with six or more colors of ink, rather than the standard four, will print much better in highlight areas, and tonal gradations will be smoother and more refined. This option is standard on high-end printers but only starting to appear on less expensive models.

Ink cartridges Be sure to do price comparisons on ink costs before making your purchase; the inks can make more of a dent in your budget than the cost of the printer! Ink cartridges start at $12 to $15; for high-end printers they are about $75 each. We recommend buying a printer that allows you to replace individual colors of ink. With grouped cartridges (usually red/blue/yellow), you must replace the whole set of colors if one color runs out, which is wasteful and expensive.

INKJET INKS AND PERMANENCE

You may have heard or read that inkjet prints fade rapidly and cannot be counted on for permanence. This was quite true of early inkjet printers, but that's now changing. The biggest improvement has been in the inks themselves. There are currently two types of ink for inkjet printers: *dye-based* and *pigment-based*. They are not interchangeable because they require different print heads. When you purchase refill cartridges, always use the type of ink that came with your printer.

Here are the pros and cons of each:

Dye-based inks Standard with most inkjet printers, dye-based inks are usually water-soluble when wet and fairly water-resistant when dry. They produce strong, accurate colors and work with a wide variety of paper surfaces and textures. Unfortunately, they may lose color after a year or two, although there are some dye-based inks that are fade-resistant and last longer. Hewlett Packard now claims a life of 70-plus years for some of their dye-based inks and more are becoming available all the time.

Pigment-based inks These use organic solids suspended in either an oil- or water-based matrix. When the pigmented ink is sprayed onto a paper surface, the pigment particles remain long after the water or oil has dried. A big advance in permanence for inkjet users, pigmented inks are expected to last from 50 to 200 years without fading. Epson's pigment-based inks are designed to last up to 75 years. Currently these are more expensive as well.

Paper thickness   Look carefully at the paper path capabilities. If you want to print on a thicker paper, fabric, or card stock—which you will—be sure the printer adjusts for paper thickness. Some printers will also accept rolls of paper to make long prints (panoramas) or banners.

Print size   Consider carefully what size prints you want to make. Most printers can handle 8½- x 11-inch paper, but if you want larger prints, the next size up accepts 12- or 13-inch-wide sheets. When you really think big (and that includes your budget), high-end printers start at 17 inches wide. Most of you will need to source out your oversize printing to a local copy shop or service bureau.

Print speed   Unless your printer has its own memory card, print speed is determined mostly by your computer's processing speed and available RAM (random access memory). Compare manufacturers' claims for printing times using the BEST setting in the PRINT dialog box rather than the SPEED setting, as this is what you'll be using.

Resolution   Printer resolution is not the same as image file resolution. For more information, see page 19. Very high printer resolution improves the printer's ability to render detail. Look for a printer that offers at least 1440 x 720 dpi (dots per inch), which will give a true photo quality to the print. Printers with less resolution, though, will still print very acceptable photos.

LASER PRINTERS

A laser printer (and photocopier) uses powdered color toner rather than ink to produce an image. The toner first adheres to the charged areas of the drum and is then heated, which fuses a permanent image on the paper. Because of the matte quality of toner, the color of a laser print is less intense than one produced by an inkjet printer. Thanks to extensive research in the field of toner-based printing, big strides are being made in the quality and competitiveness of laser printers. Models for the home user that print letter size are already available and comparably priced to inkjet.

PHOTOCOPIERS

All of us photocrafters used color copy machines for years before the digital revolution came along to eclipse them. If you don't own a printer of any kind, you can still make many of the projects in this book by copying, resizing, or otherwise manipulating your images on a copier at your local copy shop. Just remember that these will be toner-based prints, like those from a laser printer. Be sure to use the paper and fabric stock appropriate for laser technology.

Color photocopiers are digital and work much like a scanner that is connected to a laser printer. The scanning element in the copier scans the image in color and then transfers it via laser to a charged image drum before printing it in the same manner as a color laser printer. High-end machines apply all four colors in a single application. Low-end copiers require four passes across the image.

IMAGE-EDITING SOFTWARE

Do you wish your dog looked larger in that close-up? Do you want to add yourself to the class reunion photo? Turn your favorite snapshot into a dramatic black-and-white poster? Enlarge an image so it's two feet wide or shrink it to two inches square? With image-editing software, you can do it all, plus so much more. This almost magical software lets you easily resize, recolor, or rearrange your pictures in countless ways, and do it again and again to achieve amazing effects.

This is important, so it's worth repeating (in case you missed it in How to Use This Book): We chose ADOBE PHOTOSHOP ELEMENTS 4.0 as the image-editing software for the projects in this book. We recommend it, not only because it will make following project instructions exponentially easier but because, as of this writing, it is by far the best basic image-editing program out there. It's easy to learn, fun to play with, and readily available for under $80.

No matter which software you use, our best advice is this: Get comfortable with its basic features before you start any serious project. Play around. Don't be afraid to really alter your images. If you hate the results, you can always hit DELETE. That's how you'll learn the program. You'll have more fun if you don't push yourself to master every feature perfectly. That said, if you don't already know them, please take the time now to learn these ten critical image-editing features in ELEMENTS (or their equivalents in your program). They will crop up again and again throughout the projects, and are an essential part of your photocraft repertoire. Practice now for better photocraft later!

10 IMAGE-EDITING ESSENTIALS FOR YOUR PHOTOCRAFT TOOL KIT

Master these ten features, and you'll be able to do *a lot:*

• **Clone stamp tool** Select one area of your image and then "clone" it onto another area. Sound helpful? It's great for removing dirt and hair, and for repairing damaged images.

• **Color controls** Allows you to make subtle or major color changes, including altering hue, saturation, adjusting color cast, and even replacing colors.

• **Cropping tool** You'll undoubtedly use this often to change the dimensions of your photo, or to keep the best parts of your image and remove the rest.

• **Cut, copy, and paste** One of the most basic and useful features of your software, it works much the same as in your word-processing application.

• **Image size** A critical feature that lets you adjust the size and/or resolution of your image, as well as enabling you to resample your image either up or down.

• **Layers** When you open your photograph in ELEMENTS it will have only one layer—the background. To this, you can add additional layers containing type, color, shapes, and other images. Imagine all these things on layers of clear acetate, stacked one on top of another. Together, they make up the image. Layers are a great tool because you can work on one individually without affecting the rest.

- **Levels** Adjusts the dark, light, and midtones separately, allowing for precise control over the brightness and contrast of your image.

- **Selection tools** (MARQUEE TOOLS, LASSO TOOLS, SELECTION BRUSH, and MAGIC WAND) As their names imply, these tools allow you to "select" different parts of your image in order to delete, adjust, or cut them out without affecting the rest of your image. To choose large areas of one tone, use the MAGIC WAND. To cut out complicated shapes, try the MAGNETIC LASSO. You will often use more than one selection tool in order to complete the task.

- **Type tool** Allows you to add words and numbers in your chosen font, size, and color to an image.

- **Unsharp mask** A filter that adds contrast to make your image appear sharper.

▶ OUTSOURCING

There may be times when you want to blow up an image to billboard size, scan in 400 pictures from grandma's album, or print an image onto vinyl or canvas. If you can't do it with your home equipment, there are professionals waiting to help you complete almost any photocraft project imaginable.

Service bureaus and photo labs
Primarily serving the professional photographic, graphic arts, and printing industries, service bureaus typically have drum scanners, larger flatbed scanners, and wide-format printers that can produce scans and prints of much better resolution than any home equipment. A photo lab will develop and print film both from negatives and from digital files, enlarge them to any size, do retouching, make scans, and print them on canvas and specialty papers.

Using a service bureau or photo lab is likely to be a relatively expensive choice, but the quality of their work will be very high. Several projects in this book require their services. Check the yellow pages under "Desktop Publishing & Service Bureaus," "Computer Graphics & Digital Imaging," or "Photo Finishing-Retail." Before making a project that will be subject to water, sunlight, or weathering (such as Shower Curtain, page 150), don't hesitate to call local service bureaus or photo labs and ask a sales rep to explain the choices and differences between their digital and traditional prints.

Copy shops
Your local copy shop, copy chains such as Kinko's, and the neighborhood "Quick Print" shop offer a good and less expensive alternative to service bureaus, depending on the level of quality and expertise you need. Copy shops offer numerous, invaluable services: All have color copiers and most have the ability to scan images, burn them onto CDs, make large-size prints, laminate, and print on banner rolls or heavier stock. Some handle unusual materials like backlit film and vellum or equipment like heat presses; others have scanners and printers you can rent by the hour. In addition they will copy, trim, collate, punch, staple, and bind for you. Each shop will vary in the services offered, so shop around or ask friends in the creative arts for their recommendations.

THE MATERIAL WORLD

YOU NOW HAVE ALL THESE WONDERFUL IMAGES. What will you print them on? And how do you cut them? Glue them? Seal them? Frame them? And otherwise turn them into finished photocraft masterpieces?

⚠ **A caution about materials:** Regardless of how much information we give you, always read the manufacturer's instructions and safety precautions before you begin any project. There may be quirks associated with the usage of that particular brand. More important, many adhesives and sealants (particularly spray sealants) smell horrendous, are toxic to breathe, and/or can be fatal if swallowed. Some can severely irritate your skin. Take the label precautions seriously and always be sure to use these materials only in well-ventilated areas, and, if recommended, with a ventilator mask.

▶ PAPER

Today's vast selection of papers is what really fuels the digital-inkjet revolution. Now that you can print at home on almost any stock (as opposed to being stuck solely with glossy photo paper), digital art can be as tactile, exciting, and innovative as lithography, etching, collage, even painting. You'll be amazed at the effect a simple change of paper can make to the look and feel of your images.

Choices range from inexpensive machine-made papers for projects with brief life spans to higher quality artist's papers to archival handmade papers, which are the longest lasting. At any level of quality, we recommend the use of papers coated specifically for inkjet or laser use. Even the least expensive of these will produce outstanding image quality from your printer. Paper companies occasionally offer their wares in sample packs, a good way to get to know their different characteristics.

Trial and error is the best way to learn how particular papers interact with your printer, how different stocks take ink, and what effects you can get from playing around with different images and settings. For optimal results, be sure to match the media settings in your PRINT dialog box (like PLAIN PAPER, BRIGHT WHITE INKJET, GLOSSY PHOTO PAPER) to the paper type you are using. A variety of textures and surfaces are now available, so experiment and compare. Eventually focus on one or two types of paper. That way you can be sure of consistent results.

GENERAL PAPERS

Paper companies are working hard to provide a wide range of paper usable with both inkjet and laser/toner technology. In many cases you will find that your favorite papers are interchangeable, but in some cases, particularly with specialty papers, only one type of printer will be compatible. Be sure to read the package label to confirm that it meets your needs before buying.

Copy paper and letterhead stock Inexpensive photocopy paper and colored letterhead stock, available in 20 lb. and 24 lb. weights, are usually made with wood pulp that has been neutralized to some degree. It is rarely archival, but will do fine for many of the projects in this book (after all, does it matter if a party invitation yellows a year after the party?). Use copy paper to test enlargements and compositions while image-editing; switch to the good stuff to color correct and print your final image.

Bristol board Sold under many names, including card stock, poster paper, and cover stock, Bristol board is slightly heavier than copy paper and has a smooth finish. It will feed through any printer that adjusts for paper thickness. Use it for business cards, tags, sturdy envelopes, small boxes, or signs. Bristol board is often the choice for printed material that requires repeated handling.

Standard photo papers If you don't specify something else, this is what your local copy shop or office supply store will use to print your images. Like copy paper and letterhead, these are also made from wood pulp. While perfectly fine for many of the projects in this book, we encourage you to upgrade whenever you can afford to, especially for labor-intensive and/or tactile projects like a book or folding screen, note cards, art prints—anything you plan to frame or display and hope to preserve. You will see a qualitative difference. Choose heavier weight photo papers (50 lb. to 65 lb.) for projects with heavy ink coverage.

High-quality fine art papers The next level up in both longevity and price are archival, machine-made photo papers, often referred to as fine art papers or "artist's" papers. The best of these are the 100% cotton, coated inkjet papers made by Hahnemühle, Lumijet, Somerset, Epson, Rives, and Arches, to name just a few in a rapidly growing selection. See "Our Favorite High Quality Papers," page 32, for some specific recommendations. Art supply stores and print shops may carry a small selection. You will get the best selection and prices by ordering these online.

Handmade papers Great permanence is one characteristic of truly made-by-hand papers. These archival rag papers are made one sheet at a time using all-cotton pulp free of any chemical agents. As with anything hand-crafted, each sheet will be slightly unique. Many handmade papers have a great deal of texture to them; others have embedded flower petals, threads, or embossing. You can find handmade papers at most high-end art supply stores.

▶ **TIP** Prior to 1900, most paper was manufactured of cotton, which is acid-free and can conceivably last forever. Today, however, paper is primarily made of wood pulp, which is naturally high in acid content. Over time, acid breaks down paper's structure, causing it to become dark and brittle. Acid-free papers and materials contain no acid or have had the acid removed so they have a more neutral pH. Seriously consider using acid-free materials on any prints or projects you want to last a lifetime. However, keep in mind that other factors besides the acidity of the paper, such as ink chemistries and display conditions, may affect the image permanence of inkjet prints. But you add longevity to any project by printing it on archival paper stock.

OUR FAVORITE HIGH QUALITY PAPERS

For ambitious projects, or ones that you will frame and display, don't skimp on paper quality. Use a high quality paper. You will get a return from your investment in improved results and greater longevity. All of these except the Japanese papers come in numerous cut-sheet sizes as well as rolls. Here are a few we've tried and like.

Medium weight

Crane Museo Very smooth, archival, and high quality. A slightly off-white paper that renders excellent color and shadow detail.

Crane Museo Silver Rag This beautiful new rag paper with the feel of a fine cotton paper has outstanding tonal range and color depth. For use with pigmented inks.

Epson Matte Heavyweight A good, less-expensive paper for proofing; not archival.

Hahnemühle Photo Rag A bright white, 100% cotton-rag, acid-free paper designed especially for optimum photographic reproduction. Works equally well with both dye and pigment inks. Available in five different weights.

Somerset Photo Enhanced A beautiful surface that yields good contrast, excellent detail, and rich colors. Brighter white than many other art papers. It is one of the most versatile of all the inkjet-ready papers. **Somerset Velvet** is the same paper, but uncoated.

Heavyweight

Epson Enhanced Matte Poster Board A thick poster-board with a smooth surface. If your printer accepts thicker sheets, using this stock will save you mounting the printed image.

Hahnemühle German Etching Board 310 A beautiful, heavy paper that yields a very nice printed black. Requires a printer that can handle ultra-heavyweight stock. Also sold as **Lumijet Classic Velour** and **Lyson Standard Fine Art Watercolor Paper.**

Legion Photo Matte A heavyweight paper that looks and feels uncoated but due to a special matte coating yields great detail, outstanding contrast, and high color resolution. Works equally as well with both dye-based and pigmented inks on a wide variety of printers. One of our favorites, we used it for our folding screen, page 145.

Special surfaces

Hahnemühle Albrecht Durer 210 A rough-textured watercolor paper with a warm white tone. The surface is tough and the coating was designed to minimize image fading. Also sold as **Lumijet Flaxen Weave** and **Lyson Rough Fine Art Paper.**

Japanese Kinwashi Made from hemp and Kozo fibers. A very translucent, decorative paper, slightly golden hued, treated for inkjet printing.

Japanese Kozo-Shi A thin, strong paper the color of unbleached muslin.

Japanese Warahan-Shi A slightly more yellow, medium-weight paper with one smooth side and one coarse side, for laser printers as well as inkjets.

SPECIALTY PAPERS

There are innumerable fancy and unusual papers available, many of which are now printer-friendly. Here are just a few we had fun using.

Fuzzy paper Suitable for inkjet prints, this soft, textured paper looks and feels flocked (think "old Victorian wallpaper"), adding a further dimension to images printed on it. An easy way to make your baby pictures warm and . . . fuzzy!

Inkjet Ultra Cling Comes in clear or backed with white. Simply print on the front surface, peel off the backing and adhere to card stock, book covers, invitations, envelopes, glass, or wood. Great for window decorations and jar labels. When it is time to remove the label it can be peeled safely off almost any surface.

Iron-on photo transfer paper Easy-to-find, easy-to-use photo transfer paper turns your boring old iron into an indispensable craft tool. With your home printer and a hot iron you can add lilies to a silk scarf, baby shoes to a handmade quilt, or your dog's lovable mug to a holiday card. There are many brands; some work better than others. Be sure to read "Achieving Great Results with Iron-On Transfer Paper," page 37, so you know which kind to buy.

Holographic Papers These come in bright, matte, cracked ice, and glitter finishes, among others, which give the resulting print a unique, multidimensional appearance. Perfect for invitations to a rock 'n' roll party!

Magnetic sheets Inkjet printable magnet sheets can be run through your printer just like inkjet paper. Simply print, cut apart, and stick on your fridge, or mail to adoring grandparents! Also ideal for save-the-date invitations or a kitchen calendar.

Metallic-coated papers You'll find gold, silver, and pearl finishes available for inkjet printers. These materials add unusual depth to photographs. Give your image the look of an old sepia photograph by printing it on gold paper, or give it a bronze glow by tinting the background of your image orange, then printing it on silver stock. Pearl paper has a lovely matte iridescence that resembles satin.

Self-adhesive paper A box of 8½- x 11-inch sheets from your local office supply store is the most economical, but you'll also find this paper sold by the sheet at art supply stores. The paper backing peels off, exposing the adhesive coating. Depending on where you buy it, it's also sold as peel-off label paper, adhesive paper, or adhesive-backed paper. Full-page adhesive sheets that you can cut to a custom size are the most versatile. You'll find label paper in a range of sizes per sheet, another option if you find a ready-cut label that suits your project. If you have a Xyron Sticker Maker or Daige Rollataq Hand Applicator, you can add an adhesive backing to practically any paper.

Silver self-adhesive film Treated for inkjet printing with a peel-off backing, this film has a brilliant silver mirror finish on one side that is great for creating special effects. We used it for one of our note cards (For a Big Birthday, page 71).

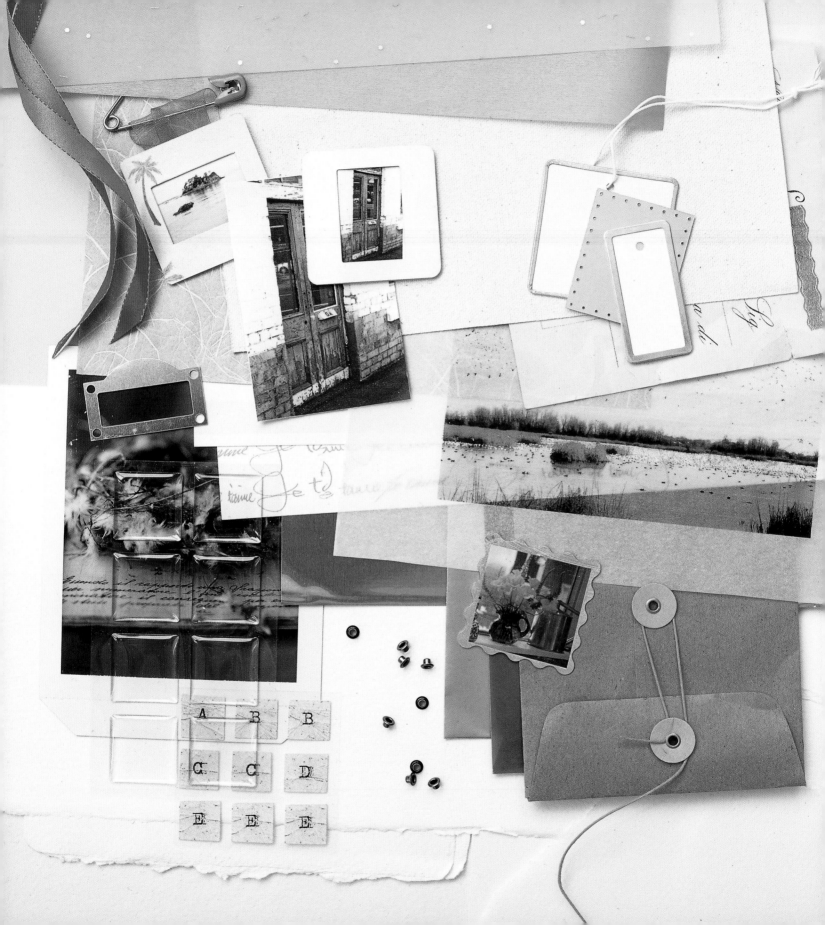

Vellum paper A very thin and elegant paper with a hard surface, vellum has a translucency that is extremely appealing but prevents inks from penetrating. Because the ink sits on the paper's surface, it may crackle or blur, so be sure to test various brands of vellum to find one that works with the inks you prefer. Various online paper suppliers carry vellums they have pretested and guarantee to work. Or pick up a box at an office supply, art, or craft store and do your own testing.

GETTING THE BEST RESULTS FROM YOUR PAPER

Now that you've gone digital, paper will be one of your biggest expenses. Using the correct paper in the right way will save you time and money, and reduce frustration. Consider the following when you choose a stock for your project.

Absorbency Inkjet papers are coated to prevent the ink from soaking into the paper and bleeding onto neighboring colors. If you must run a paper through your printer that is not specifically coated for inkjet printing, first check its absorbency by testing a small area with drops of water and colored inks. Also, be aware that chemicals in the pulp and ink on old papers can have adverse chemical reactions that will affect the look of your print.

Color Colored stocks are often beautiful and can greatly alter the mood or presentation of an ordinary image. Keep in mind that the image highlights will be the color of the paper you choose. White or off-white paper will give you the truest whites in your image as well as enhancing the color range of your inks.

Paper thickness Know what papers can go through your printer. Very thick or thin papers may jam, catch and wrap around the rollers, or misalign your print heads. When testing papers of varying thicknesses, pay attention to the loading procedures for your printer. Some of the newer printers can accept very thick papers, including poster board. Thin papers can be taped to a thicker sheet and passed through the printer, but proceed with caution!

Print on the correct side To get the right results, it's very important to print on the front or coated side of a piece of paper. But it can be a challenge to tell which side is coated. Most paper packaging has a sticker that tells you, usually the side facing up when you open the box. Sometimes color difference is a clue: The front side is whiter than the back, which may look yellowish or off-white.

Permanence If you find a paper that you want to use regularly you can research its permanence–how long it will maintain quality–through Wilhelm Imaging Research, Inc., a company devoted to research, consulting, and publications on the permanence and light-fastness of photographic and digital materials. Check their Web site (www.wilhelm-research.com) for the latest updates.

ACHIEVING GREAT RESULTS WITH IRON-ON TRANSFER PAPER

Choose the proper paper

Transparent and opaque You'll find transfer papers sold as transparent (also labeled "clear") and opaque; if the package doesn't specify, then it's probably transparent. With transparent papers, what is white in your photograph will lack pigment when printed, allowing the grain and color of the material you fuse it to (wood, cloth, paper) to show through. For example, if you print on ivory or tan, you can give your image the look of a vintage sepia print. Opaque transfer paper, on the other hand, eliminates show-through by backing the entire image with white; it works best for transfers onto dark colors. For the projects in this book, we specify which type to use. All transfer papers, however, leave a coating of the transfer medium, which may have a waxy or plastic texture.

For porous and nonporous materials Most transfer papers are specifically designed for use with either porous (paper, raw wood, cloth) or nonporous (tile, metal, painted wood, glass) materials. Newer ones are now available that work with a lower heat setting so images can be transferred to vinyl and plastic. The nonporous materials, however, will not absorb the inks and are also harder to do successfully. (Then again, your transfer "failure" could end up being more interesting than a perfectly transferred image.)

For inkjet and color laser Both inkjet printers and color laser printers (that includes photocopiers) can accept transfer paper. However, the transfer papers for the two processes are not interchangeable; be sure you have the one that is correct for your equipment.

• • • • • • • • •

A 16-year-old with little sewing skill made this remarkable album quilt as a Mother's Day gift. She printed her own scans of family photos onto fabric transfer sheets and fused them to the squares with an iron after the quilt was pieced together.

Choose the proper material

Smooth finish The smoother the surface and the finer its grain, the better the image will transfer. If it is transferred over a bumpy surface the image will be stretched over the lumps and bumps and distorted—which might or might not be a wonderful look. If you are transferring onto fabric, its thread count should be at least 200 threads per inch.

Heat resistant The standard heat setting for transfers is 300–375 degrees F (Cotton/Linen, or HIGH). Be sure you use a material that can withstand this temperature, or use a transfer paper designed to work at lower heat settings.

No wrinkles or steam Don't use an ironing board; it's too soft. A pillowcase or a clean, wrinkle-free cloth laid over a wooden cutting board or set on the kitchen counter makes an ideal ironing surface for transfers. Don't use a steam setting, as moisture interferes with the transfer process.

Use proper care If the garment needs ironing later, don't iron directly on the image transfer. Protect the image with a silicone- or Teflon-coated ironing cloth, or iron on the reverse side. To retain maximum sharpness and color, garments with transfers should be hand washed or washed inside out in the washing machine in warm water and laid flat to dry. Do not use bleach or fabric softener.

Choose the right photo

The transfer process softens details and reduces contrast. If you want a crisp final image, start with photos that are in sharp focus with good contrast. You may need to increase brightness, contrast, and/or saturation with your image-editing software to get the desired result. Image resolution needs to be fairly high—300 or 350 dpi is preferred.

FABRICS

Today's printable fabrics are incredibly diverse, vibrantly colored, washable, and dry-cleanable, making it easy to incorporate photographs into photocraft projects. Piece an heirloom quilt using printable cotton or iron-on fabric transfers. Craft a doll whose face is your daughter's photo. Stitch a washable tablecloth for the picnic table. Personalize the bedroom curtains. Create wearable or frame-worthy fabric art. Printable fabrics are the foundation for all of these projects. The types and weights of silks, in particular, will inspire you to incorporate fabrics in your artwork.

Paper-backed fabrics In order to run fabric through a printer, it needs to be stiffened to handle like paper, accomplished via a peel-off paper backing that is applied to the fabric at the factory. Cotton, silk, and artist's canvas are available in both sheets and rolls of various weights already prepared with this backing (which you remove after printing). In addition to stiffening the fabric, the backing also holds down edge threads that could otherwise unravel and wrap themselves around your printer's gears. Similar backed fabrics are available for use with laser printers and photocopiers, but the two kinds (inkjet and laser) are not interchangeable; again, be sure you have the product that is right for your equipment.

Artist's canvas Available in a range of textures and weights, artist's canvas is stiff enough to run through a printer without the support of paper backing. You'll find it in sheets (for printing at home) and on rolls (which require the large-format printers found at service bureaus). A photograph printed on canvas has a unique look that imbues the normally flat photographic image with the subtle texture of woven cloth. The results are beautiful, and we think worth the extra effort (see Kitchen Clock, page 131). Expect an image printed on canvas to have slightly less detail than on smooth paper. Prints on canvas are fairly fragile until completely dry; give them at least 24 hours of drying time to avoid smears, then spray with Bulldog Ultra Coating before handling further.

WORKING WITH PRINTABLE FABRICS

• If you find that blacks look gray, you may get better results by switching your black ink cartridge from matte black (the standard supplied) to photo black.

• You'll get crisper images if you print on fabrics with tighter weaves; the tighter the weave, the better the image. Tightness of weave is even more important to image quality than fabric weight.

• Be sure to set your printer for envelope or card stock thickness. If your printer does not adjust for thickness, you will be restricted to lighter weight backed fabrics.

• Inkjet ink will take longer to dry on fabric than paper so handle freshly printed fabric carefully to ensure that you don't smear the image while it is drying. To be safe, allow it to dry overnight.

• Some fabrics require steaming to set the inks and assure a colorfast image; be sure to follow the product instructions. Once steamed, the printed image will hold up in use.

GLUES & ADHESIVES

Technically speaking, glues are natural and adhesives are synthetic. As a rule of thumb for choosing the right one for the task, consider the materials that are being joined and the strength of the bond needed. Glues and adhesives fall into two categories: general purpose glues and adhesives, appropriate for many common materials, and special purpose glues and adhesives that work only with specific materials. In general, don't feel compelled to buy expensive, acid-free or archival glues and adhesives; once the water evaporates, an acid glue becomes pH neutral, so there's minimal chance it will damage your artwork. Pay more attention to what harm the glue might do to you.

⚠ **Epoxy** A two-component system, epoxy consists of resin and hardener. When mixed together, they create a durable, permanent, high-strength bond for a variety of porous and nonporous materials. Be sure you mix the two components thoroughly. Most epoxies are water- and heat-resistant. For wood, PC-Woody Epoxy can be stained and sanded, and makes a waterproof wood-to-wood bond.

⚠ **Rubber- and solvent-based adhesives** This very useful category has a very major drawback: These adhesives are cumulatively toxic, meaning they accumulate in your system with prolonged exposure. Always use them in a well-ventilated area. They also degrade fairly quickly. If an adhesive has a toxicity warning on the label, it is likely to be rubber- or solvent-based. Two of the most common are rubber cement and spray mount/spray adhesive. Silicone adhesives also fall under this category; they function as both adhesives and sealers and work well in situations where the bond might get wet. Common brands include Amazing Goop, Crafters Goop, and E6000 Adhesive.

The best way to avoid this hazard is to stock nontoxic alternatives in your studio. Even if you do very little mounting, a Xyron Sticker Maker or Daige Rollataq Hand Applicator is a worthwhile investment; either can be had for under $20. They offer a simple-to-use system that rolls on a clear, microthin adhesive film that is odorless, nontoxic, and will not soak through your paper. Another option is Memory Mount, which for decades has been used by professionals for archival mounting. It is a reversible, vegetable-based liquid that can be spread as a thin film, and will not wrinkle even thin tissue.

Vegetable paste Typically, this is made from wheat starch, potato starch, rice, seaweed, or other natural plant materials. Very archival and totally reversible, it is the choice for many conservation uses. It washes off hands and clothing easily, is acid-free, and nontoxic. The downside is that the paste is edible to insects that can eat through your artwork or backing to get to it. You'll find this product sold as Wheat Paste, Yes Glue, Coccoina Paste, Nori Paste, Yamato Sticking Paste.

Weld-on adhesives Plastics are tricky because there are so many types and they all have different properties. Weld-on Products makes a line of products specifically formulated for gluing all types of plastics.

White craft glue Ordinary white glue, also known as PVA (polyvinyl acetate), is undoubtedly the most versatile all-purpose adhesive for crafts. Nontoxic, odorless, and nonflammable, it dries clear in under an hour and cleans up with warm water. These glues are designed to work with porous materials only, making them ideal for paper, wood, cloth, cardboard, and more. The bond is reversible, so they aren't water resistant, however. White glues are very inert when dry, making a stable bond over the short term. As they age, however, cheaper versions will become brittle and more prone to cracking. You find them under brand names such as Elmer's, Aleene's Tacky Glue, Grrrip Glue, Crafter's Pick Incredibly Tacky, and Dala Craft Glue.

For greater stability and permanence, consider using one of the higher grade acetate adhesives, as they will remain flexible over time. Any white glue that says it will bond plastics is likely to be in this category. If you want projects to last, we recommend using Crafter's Pick "The Ultimate" or Crafter's Pick 1100 Bookbinding Glue. These will glue ceramics, glass, leather, and some plastic and metal surfaces as well as porous materials. Another choice is Sobo Premium Craft and Fabric Glue.

Adhesive remover With acid-free un-du Adhesive Remover or Adhesive Eraser, it's quick and easy to remove misplaced adhesive from projects. Either will strip all Xyron adhesive residue and most others.

▶ FINISHING TOUCHES

Now that you've made a masterpiece, how do you protect it? Color laser and inkjet prints are susceptible to damage from pollutants in the air, ultraviolet (UV) light, and water, and need protection from dust, insects, and sticky fingers. There are various materials and methods for protecting artwork, some are reversible and many are permanent. Carefully consider what you may want to undo in the future before choosing a permanent option.

PROTECTIVE SPRAYS AND COATINGS

Prints framed under UV-inhibiting glass or sheet acrylic plastic (Plexiglas) don't need to be protected with a surface coating. But prints that are framed under normal glass or left exposed to the air—used in a calendar, or printed on canvas, for example—should be protected, both to inhibit fading and to give the print some resistance to water, dirt, and fingerprints. Remember to apply these products in well-ventilated areas and always read the safety information first. Here are some of our favorites:

⚠ **Bulldog Ultra Coating** Designed to protect ink on canvas, Bulldog has a vinyl base that makes it flexible and prevents the inks from cracking when the print is handled. It blocks UV light, makes the prints waterproof, and is nonyellowing.

Genesis Inkset Clear Giclée Gloss Coating A nontoxic, odorless, acid-free, and flexible top-coat sealant with UV absorbers and light stabilizers that is brushed on. For use with all water-based inkjet media. Surfaces coated with Inkset can be cleaned with dish soap and water.

Golden Archival Varnish One of the better choices for UV resistance, this solvent-based, acrylic liquid produces a flexible, clear film that will protect against environmental threats such as dirt and moisture, and can be reversed with mineral spirits. Apply a minimum of two coats with a brush.

⚠️ **Krylon Preserve It! Paper Protectant** Contains UV absorbers and inhibitors and is specifically made for paper and digital prints. Krylon UV Resistant Coating works well for other materials, such as metal and wood, but not for paper. As with all sprays be sure to wear a mask and work in a well-ventilated area.

⚠️ **Lyson Print Guard** This spray works very well for ink on paper. It makes prints more resistant to moisture, has a UV inhibitor that improves resistance to fading, and is nonyellowing. A good choice for fine art prints. A similar product is **Lumijet Image Shield**.

⚠️ **Mona Lisa Clear Cote Liquid** You'll get a more permanent coating with this product, which dries quickly to a very high gloss porcelain finish that does not yellow. It works on paper, wood, metal, plaster, and glass. One of the best products on the market, its downside is that it is quite toxic and you will need a mask and well-ventilated area when you use it.

MULTIPURPOSE SEALERS

A number of products on the market can be used for all tasks: sealing a porous surface before applying paint or photos, adhering materials onto the base material, and adding a protective coating for the finished piece. Most are water-based and nontoxic, and can be brushed on over wood, paper, cardboard, canvas, acrylic paints, fabric, and more.

Acrylic medium/acrylic gel medium/acrylic matte (or gloss) medium These are all names for the acrylic polymer emulsion that is the basic building block for making all kinds of acrylic paint, sold in tubes, pints, or quarts at art supply stores. It works moderately well as an adhesive and beautifully for decoupage or for putting a protective finish coat on your artwork. Dries clear, but multiple coats over dark colors may have a slight whitish tint. It is not removable once it dries. A very inexpensive, all-purpose glue and sealer.

Liquid Laminate Nontoxic and nonflammable, it adheres to most smooth surfaces including glass, wood, cardboard, plastic, metal, and polymer clay. Great for decoupage, it dries crystal clear with a glossy shine and is water and UV resistant when multiple coats are applied. Once dried, it is removable with ammonia or alcohol.

Mod Podge A favorite for decoupage, this is another glossy sealer for protecting and finishing projects. It is not as hard or as clear as Mona Lisa Clear Cote Spray but it's easy to clean up.

Omni-Gel This transfer medium is available in both gloss and matte finishes. It can be used to laminate and waterproof prints as well as for transferring photo imagery (see Faux Tintype Jewelry, page 107).

Royal Coat Antique Decoupage Finish Use this decoupage paste, available in clear satin and antique finishes, to make your artwork look aged. It yellows when it dries; the more you apply, the more yellow it gets.

LAMINATION

Laminating machines apply a thin plastic film over the top, or top and bottom of your art, and seal it around the edges, protecting it from food and drink, accidental smudges, and rough handling, as well as stiffening it for greater strength. It's a terrific choice for protecting your photographs under a variety of conditions. There are two basic types of lamination—hot and cold. If one type isn't suitable for a particular artwork, the other likely is. Keep in mind, however, that both types are permanent and nonreversible so lamination is not a good choice for unique artwork or valuable photographs. Unless you own a home laminator, you can usually have your projects laminated at a local copy shop.

Cold lamination This process passes the image between rollers, and bonds the lamination by means of pressure. Xyron home laminating machines are the best known, but many other brands are now available. They require no electricity, are usable immediately (no downtime while the machine heats up), and are compatible with all types of printed media. Many will accept materials that are slightly uneven such as embossed paper or pressed flowers; they are a good choice if you have incorporated in your artwork any materials that are heat sensitive, such as crayons. These machines will laminate one side, both sides, or apply adhesive to one side and lamination to the other—a great bonus if you are making labels. However, as the coating offers no UV resistance, don't expect it to protect your work from fading.

Hot lamination A great choice for signs, place mats, calendars, and similar crafts. It laminates your photograph very securely between two layers of film, using either pouches or rolls of plastic laminate (available in several thicknesses). The heat will not alter your photograph, but the coating can't be removed. We've had better luck laminating photos with matte rather than gloss finish. Most hot laminators can only handle very specific thicknesses, and you will need to leave a border of laminate around the artwork in order to keep it sealed. Film that offers some UV protection is available for hot laminators.

Iron-on vinyl (like Iron-On Flexible Vinyl from Therm O Web) is a variation of hot lamination. The material is sold by the yard in a 17-inch width at hobby and fabric stores, with either matte or shiny finish, and ironed on at home with an ordinary household iron. Use it to protect one or both sides of cotton fabrics that are too large or too thick to go through a laminating machine. (We used this product for Pet Place Mats and the baby bib variation, pages 81–83). Because it sets at a lower temperature, the bond is not as permanent as one from a hot-laminating machine.

FRAMING YOUR IMAGES

We wrote *Photocraft* to forever banish shoeboxes stuffed with images soon forgotten or dusty albums that never get looked at. You've created digital art worthy of display whether you give it pride of place on the coffee table or give it away as a gift. A classic mat and frame is one of the nicest ways to finish an image. Whether you do the work yourself or use a professional, it's always preferable to use high-quality, non-acidic materials.

Frames Should you use wood or metal frames? The choice is more aesthetic than practical. Metal frames often cost less and are easily assembled at home if ordered cut to size. Wood frames can be warm and elegant. You can buy ready-made wood frames in a variety of standard sizes that, if carefully chosen, can look as elegant as a custom-cut frame.

Glass versus acrylic You will quickly find that everything fades much faster if exposed to direct sunlight. It is best to use glass or acrylic that has ultraviolet (UV) filtering to reduce the damaging effects of sunlight, and fluorescent and halogen lamps. Acrylic with UV-filtering properties is more effective than UV-filtering glass. Further, acrylic won't break and is also lighter than glass, an important advantage when framing large pieces. On the other hand, acrylic is harder to clean and it scratches easily. Make sure the mat is thick enough to prevent the glass or acrylic from coming in contact with the image. If you're not using a mat, put spacers (such as thin strips of mat board) between the image and the glass to keep them from touching.

Mat board Although mat board is available in many colors, we recommend choosing a neutral color that complements your image, not overpowers it. White or antique white always works. White sets off the image, particularly graphic compositions like black-and-white photographs. When measuring for your mat, give more weight to the bottom margin since the eye reads the bottom line first. The ideal proportions are: side and top margins equal, bottom margin $\frac{1}{2}$ to 1 inch larger.

Mounting Artwork should be hinged to the backing board of the mat only at the top to allow for expansion on humid days. Never tape down or glue all four edges. Alternatively, if the edges of the artwork won't show, you can use acid-free or polyester photo corners. Other recommended materials include acid-free linen tape (also called framer's tape), or Japanese paper and wheat paste. Never use spray adhesives, rubber cement, pressure-sensitive backing, or self-adhesive tapes.

THE PHOTOCRAFT PANTRY

Now you know everything we know about computers, digital cameras, printers, scanners, and laminators; about the wealth of inspiring materials at your fingertips to create with; as well as the techniques that will help you preserve and display your finished creations. As the last step (or the first step, really), review this list of basic tools and materials. It's what we recommend you have on hand to make the projects in this book. We've expressed our preferences in some cases, but the final decisions should be yours. After completing a project or two, you'll know which best suit your own photocraft style.

For cutting

Craft knife These interchangeable small knives (like X-Acto and Snap-Off blade cutters) are indispensable for crafting and cutting. We particularly like ones that are retractable, making them both easy to use and safe to handle, as well as knives with snap-off blades—one quick motion and you have a fresh, sharp point.

Cutting mat These 18- x 24-inch sheets, made from a very resilient vinyl, are commonly referred to as "self-healing" because the plastic surface seals over again immediately after you cut on it. The grid lines on the mat help ensure that you cut at precise right angles.

Metal ruler A 24-inch-long metal ruler is versatile for everything from measuring to scoring to serving as a cutting guide for your knife or rotary cutter. A wider ruler will be easier to hold in place as you cut, preventing nicked fingers. Avoid plastic rulers, as they are easily chipped with a cutting knife.

Rotary cutter Available from fabric or craft stores, it has a circular rolling blade that cuts without pulling. We prefer this tool over craft knives for cutting delicate papers or fabrics. And if you have a lot to cut, they prevent hand fatigue. However, they don't work well on thicker materials.

Scissors High-quality scissors are a worthwhile investment. They last longer, cut more easily, and their blades can be resharpened. Keep two pairs handy, one to be used solely for cutting paper, and one for cutting tape and coarser surfaces (covered with paint or glue, for example). Use a utility knife—not your scissors—for thicker surfaces. Be sure to have scissors sharpened periodically.

Utility knife Also known as a mat knife, it has a larger blade than a craft knife, suitable for cutting heavier materials such as mat board, cardboard, plastic, vinyl, and rubber. We prefer the retractable ones with snap-off blades.

For adhering

Glue stick Good to have on hand for small, quick glue jobs, but don't reach for a glue stick if you intend your project to become an heirloom, as the glue eventually deteriorates.

Linen tape (framer's tape) What to use for hinging mat board and mounting artwork. It is archival grade, remains stable, and is easily reversed, leaving the photograph in its original state.

Masking tape The beige stuff you've used for years can't be beat when you need to hold things together temporarily or protect an area from glue or paint, but should not be left on artwork for any duration as it becomes nonremovable. (In those cases, use archival white masking tape from the art supply store.) Available at paint stores, craft stores, and art supply stores. Find very low tack (low stick, easily removable) tape in great colors like bright blue and lime green, sold as painter's tape at most hardware stores.

Transparent tape, double-stick tape Both are sold in half-inch or three-quarter-inch widths in a dispenser. Essential in innumerable projects!

White craft glue A versatile, all-purpose adhesive sold under any one of dozens of brand names. The basic version is useful for gluing porous materials only. Other varieties are now available that will glue glass, leather, and some plastic and metal surfaces as well. See page 39 for the details.

For printing

Bristol board Postcard-weight or heavier paper falls under this category, which offers a rainbow of colors. The most common size is 8½ x 11 inches (great for note cards) or in larger 18- x 24-inch or 22- x 30-inch sheets that can be cut to fit your needs. Scrap pieces make great glue applicators. Also called card stock or cover stock.

Photo paper Sold under numerous brands, photo paper comes in glossy or matte finish and is labeled specifically for use with inkjet or laser printers. We recommend using a heavier weight (50 lb. to 65 lb.), as photographs printed on thicker stock will retain their stability even with heavy ink coverage. This paper is worth the extra cost for the return in quality. Have both glossy and matte finishes on hand for test prints (images with a lot of dark colors will look much better on glossy stock).

Standard copy paper Multipurpose (for inkjet and laser printers, as well as photocopiers), this basic paper is usually sold as 20 lb. (economy grade) or 24 lb. (whiter and more opaque). Sizes are Letter (8½ x 11 inches), Legal (8½ x 14 inches), and Ledger/Tabloid (11 x 17 inches). Stock up on the sizes that work with your printer. Include a pack of tabloid paper even if that size is too large for your printer. You'll find tabloid sheets handy for sketching, making templates, or as protective, disposable covering for work surfaces.

Other handy tools and materials

Clamps, binder clips, rubber bands, and clothespins Have an assortment available, as they're great for holding small items of a project in place while you attach other parts, and for clamping pieces together while the glue dries.

Disposable paint brushes Inexpensive brushes, such as ones with 1-inch- and 2-inch-wide heads (often called china bristle) and sponge brushes, are endlessly useful for applying primers, paints, glues, and sealants. They are actually washable and reusable but won't last many rounds.

Foam roller You'll reach for a small 3- or 4-inch-wide roller often to apply glue quickly and evenly or for smoothing out air bubbles. Rollers from hardware stores have separate handles and replaceable foam covers; rollers from craft stores usually don't come apart or accept replacement covers.

Freezer paper, waxed paper These basic pantry staples sold in rolls at the grocery store protect tables, counters, or any work surface from glue or paint. A sheet of one or the other will also keep your project pristine if it must be weighted while an adhesive sets.

Marking tools Have a variety of pencils, pens, markers, pastels, oil sticks, and colored pencils on hand so you can experiment freely.

Small pliers, tweezers Needle-nose pliers are essential for framing and assembling, and a pair of large tweezers eases the task of arranging small items into a collage.

> ## *Metric conversion chart*
>
> **1 inch** = 2.54 cm (or 25.4 mm)
> **1 foot** = 30.48 cm (or .3048 m)
> **1 yard** = 91.44 cm (or .9144 m)

that they called Sarah Ann.

PHOTO PLAY

2.

Learn While You Create

PHOTO
TRANSFERS

Use a photo transfer to transform a plain "something" in your wardrobe into something special. It's easy. Print the image onto fabric transfer paper. Then heat set it with the same iron that you use to press out the wrinkles in your shirt. The first step: Read "Achieving Great Results with Iron-On Transfer Paper," page 37.

TANK TOPS

Banish boring boxy t-shirts! One great thing about iron-on transfers is that you can apply them to styles you'd actually wear. And you can tailor images to a special occasion or interest. Make custom tees for your college or family reunion, for your kayaking buddy (we added "5:30 A.M."–Caroline's favorite time on the water–with image-editing software), or just for you. We love the see-through effect on the orange shirt, achieved with translucent transfer paper, heated just a little longer than usual. Always test first, though, on a scrap of fabric. For dark colors, use opaque transfer paper.

BAND SHIRT

Give your band some cool exposure. For this shirt, we used the MAGNETIC LASSO to excise the band members from their original background (see Your Own Andy Warhol, page 84, for more on using selection tools to cut out portions of an image), added type (see Kids' Party Invitations, page 67, to learn how to use the TYPE tool), and gave the image an overall graphic look with the POSTERIZE command (explore other FILTERS and EFFECTS in your image-editing software for different treatments). It isn't a must, but we used opaque iron-on transfer paper to impart a bolder, more vinyl-like sheen to the image, which felt right for the band.

KITCHEN APRON

All work and no play makes an apron dull, too. We've dressed up ours with a kitschy iron-on transfer image, sized to fit over the pocket. It has a fun food theme, but you can adapt the aprons to the recipients or their passions. They're a great gift for a favorite gardener, artist, carpenter, or barbecue-loving boss. For deep-colored fabrics like this, use opaque iron-on transfer paper and follow the manufacturer's instructions exactly. If your image contains type or if you are adding it with image-editing software, you may need to flip your final artwork before you print it so it reads correctly.

THE COOLEST TISSUE BOX

IMAGES
Multiple loose photographs or printed
    digital photographs

COMPUTER TOOLS
Photocopier

PANTRY CHECKLIST
Craft knife
Cutting mat

MATERIALS
Creative Imaginations' Narratives
    Negative Strip in varying sizes
    (from craft stores)
8½- x 11-inch self-adhesive paper
Unfinished wooden tissue box
Sealer

Have you ever seen a tissue holder you really liked, much less one that's store-bought? Here's a box you'll actually love to look at because it's covered with copies of photographs that you've dug up from albums, culled from loose snapshots, or selected from photo files—a perfect, personalized gift for friends or family. It's sure to up the hipness quotient of any bathroom, bedroom, or office. Don't spend too much time arranging the photos in the negative strips (clear display folders that resemble real film negatives). It's better to carry the whole bunch to the copy shop and just start making copies.

1 The key is to organize photos in the negative strips in a somewhat random fashion. First gather a group of related images (either loose or printed at high resolution on your printer) and try different arrangements to see which compositions you like best. Go for variety: Use a combination of large, medium, and small negative strips if you have them. For an interesting effect, let a larger photo sprawl across 2 or even 3 windows on one strip.

2 Place self-adhesive paper into the manual feed of the copier. Lay 3 negative strips at a time (filled with your photos) on the glass and copy. For our box we printed 3 sheets of self-adhesive paper with images, although we suggest that you make at least 4 sheets so you have plenty of choices when you get home.

3 To cover the box, cut up strips or stick on entire sheets of images. Arrange some strips or sheets horizontally, some vertically. Trim away any pieces that overhang the edges of the box or wrap them around to an adjacent side.

4 Once the box is completely covered, apply a sealer to all surfaces to protect it.

PLAY Experiment with different kinds of imagery. Caroline used old family photos, but landscapes, flowers, or your kid's artwork could all work wonderfully. Unless you have a printer-scanner-photocopier at home, you will need to use a color photocopier from a copy shop to create these negative-strip stickers.

NO-BRAINER PHOTO BRACELETS

IMAGES
Digital images at 200 dpi resolution or
   higher

COMPUTER TOOLS
Image-editing software
Inkjet or laser printer or photocopier

PANTRY CHECKLIST
Ruler
Scissors or craft knife
Pencil

MATERIALS
Square or round, clear and colored
   mosaic stickers
Self-adhesive paper
1/2 yd. ribbon for each bracelet
Alphabet stickers, optional

Project Dimensions: Our mosaic stickers
are approx. 1 in. square.

Personalized photo bracelets mean you're never without your best friends (and vice versa). Make one. Make a bunch. They're incredibly easy to do and lots of fun to wear. Give them as very cool gifts to special people to mark an occasion or just because.

1 Measure the clear mosaic stickers. In your image-editing software, use the CROPPING bar to crop your image as you prefer and size it to be 1/4- to 1/2-inch larger than the size of your stickers (we created a 1 1/2-inch square). For best results, crop faces and objects tightly, as the final printout will be quite small.

2 Print your image onto self-adhesive paper. If you want to print more than 1 image at a time, crop and size each image you want to use and then cut and paste all of them into a new 8 1/2- x 11-inch document (make sure the resolution in the new document matches that of your digital images).

3 Center a sticker on your image, and lightly trace around it with a pencil. Cut out the image along the pencil line. Cut a piece of ribbon to fit your wrist when tied in a bow.

4 Plan your design—use multiple images, alphabet stickers to spell out words, different shapes, or plain stickers as additional decoration.

5 Now create a sandwich for each image using 2 mosaic stickers, the ribbon, and the image. First place the mosaic sticker you want as the back side, sticky side up—this can be a colored or clear one, depending on your preference. Then lay the ribbon on top of it. Peel off the paper backing from your image and lay that on top of the ribbon. Finally, place a clear mosaic sticker, sticky side down, on top of the image. Press the sandwich firmly together and let set for 1 hour. Create sandwiches with 2 color stickers around the ribbon or with alphabet stickers backed by a mosaic sticker for additional pizzazz.

PLAY We used alphabet stickers to spell out names and words on some of our bracelets. A change of colors, stickers, and ribbons will create infinite variations. That's the fun of it. If you prefer a more formal closure on your bracelet, use a clasp that you can pick up at any beading supply store.

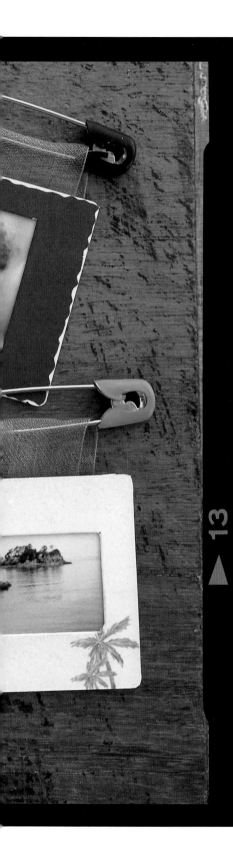

SLIDE-MOUNT PINS

We refuse to wear those tacky "Hello, My Name Is ..." paper badges. These are much more fun, totally original, and really easy! They're perfect for reunions or to break the ice when guests don't know one another and need to mingle. Simple images work best at this small scale, from how you looked "back then" to the first twig on your branch of the family tree to travel landmarks—anything that stimulates conversation or hints at identity. They make terrific gifts. Send one each month to a proud grandma to show how baby has grown.

① With your image-editing software, size and print your image, then cut out your image so it is slightly larger all around than the window of the slide mount.

② For each pin, cut a 3-inch square of decorative paper to cover the face of the slide-mount frame. Apply spray adhesive to the back of the paper square, pop open the slide mount, and press the front side of the mount onto the glue.

③ Make the window opening while the glue is still wet. Cut an X diagonally from inner corner to inner corner with a craft knife. Fold the paper around the long edges of the frame and press to adhere; trim off the points on the short side, fold over the edges, and press to

continued

IMAGES
1³⁄₈- x ⁷⁄₈-in. digital image at 300 dpi
    for each pin

COMPUTER TOOLS
Image-editing software
Inkjet or laser printer or photocopier

PANTRY CHECKLIST
Scissors
Craft knife
Cutting mat
Transparent tape
White craft glue
Small binder clip or clothespin

MATERIALS
Plastic snap-together slide mounts
    (from camera stores)
Decorative scrap paper (not card stock),
    to cover the slide mount
Spray adhesive
1¹⁄₂–2 in.-wide sheer ribbon
    (2-in. lengths per pin)
Pins, for hanging (diaper pins, blanket
    pins, or large safety pins)
White card stock, to finish the reverse
    side
Decorative trim (foil strips, stickers,
    numbers, letters), optional

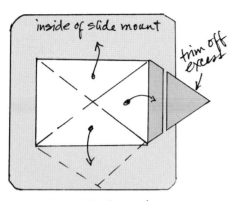

inside of slide mount

trim off excess

cut an X through the window opening, fold paper triangles to inside of slide mount.

adhere. Weight with a heavy book for 20 minutes. Once dry, trim off excess paper from the outer edges of the slide mount.

④ Trim your image so it is ⅛ inch larger all around than the opening. Position your image in the slide mount and secure it in place with small squares of tape on the inside of the slide mount.

⑤ Fold your ribbon in half around the fixed wire of your pin (the side that doesn't open; it might help to secure it with a clip). Tape the cut ends of the ribbon to the reverse side of the photo so that ½ inch of ribbon is above the slide mount. Secure the ends of the ribbon with dabs of glue, then apply glue all around the inside edge of the image, with a little extra at each corner. Close the slide mount, press it firmly together, and wipe off any glue seepage. Protect top and bottom with scrap paper and weight it with a heavy book for 30 minutes, or until the glue is thoroughly dry.

⑥ Finish the back and further secure the ribbon by gluing on a small square of white card stock that fully covers the slide mount window. Add decorative trim if desired.

"WE LOVE YOU" BEAR

THIS VERY COMFORTING, PORTABLE TEDDY BEAR MAKES A SPECIAL GET-WELL, GOING-AWAY, OR NEW BABY GIFT FOR SOME-ONE YOU HOLD DEAR. All you need is the coziest bear you can find, ribbon in cheerful colors, construction paper, and a glue stick. Cut up a contact sheet from your digital camera or photocopies made from snapshots of family and friends, and glue them to squares of construction paper. If you print or copy onto self-adhesive paper, you'll only need the glue stick to adhere the construction paper to the ribbon. If you're feeling especially creative, you can machine- or hand-stitch your assembled "portraits" to the ribbon with brightly colored thread. Long after flowers have faded, this little bear will remind its owner that he or she is very much loved.

FESTIVE VOTIVES

IMAGES
Digital images at minimum 100 dpi or
    color photocopies

COMPUTER TOOLS
Image-editing software
Inkjet or laser printer or photocopier

PANTRY CHECKLIST
Metal ruler
Rotary cutter
Cutting mat
Transparent tape
Pencil
1/2-in. double-sided or vellum tape

MATERIALS
8 1/2- x 11-in. sheets of translucent paper
    such as vellum
4 glass vases
4 votive candles (2 in. high, taller if using
    taller vases)

Project Dimensions: Our vases are 4 in.
in diameter, and 6–10 in. high.

Our custom votives glow with images printed on translucent vellum that casts a flattering pool of candlelight. They're a very quick and easy way to set the scene at any party. Wrap plain glass vases with photos of you and your partner for a romantic dinner. Light your steps with snowy scenes. Illuminate autumn color or spring blossoms. For best effect be sure to select images with strong light-and-dark contrasts or that are light overall.

1 **For each votive:** With your image-editing software, crop and size the image to fit the size of your vellum sheets. In order to fit the image around your vase, you may need to divide the image vertically and print each half on a separate sheet of paper. To do this: Make 2 copies of the original file and save them as Left-Half and Right-Half. Select the Cropping tool, and set the Cropping bar options to width = 8 1/2 inches, height = the height of your glass vase (no more than 11 inches), with resolution to match the original file. Open the Left-Half file: Start from the far left edge of the image. Select the full height of your image, crop, and save it; you will be cutting off the right edge. Open the Right-Half file: Start from the right-hand edge, crop, and save. You now have two 8 1/2- x 11-inch documents in which the image overlaps. Print each half of the image onto a separate sheet of vellum.

2 Choose an inconspicuous place in the image for the 2 halves to join. Line up your ruler along the seam line on 1 print, then cut along this line with a rotary cutter and mat. Position the trimmed half over the untrimmed half, aligning the image exactly. Temporarily tape them together on the unprinted side. Now lay the ruler along the cut seam edge of the upper sheet, and using your rotary cutter, very carefully trim the sheet below. Seam the image halves together on their back sides using transparent tape.

3 Wrap the image around the vase and mark any excess paper with a pencil so that the vertical seam, when trimmed, will meet exactly, and top and bottom edges will be flush with the edges of the vase. Be very careful that no part of the paper will be exposed to the flame of the candle. Remove the image and trim away the excess paper.

4 To affix the image to the glass, apply a strip of double-sided or vellum tape to the vase vertically, running from the top edge of the vase to the bottom. Align the image flush with the top and bottom of the vase, then press 1 vertical edge in place on half of the tape. Wrap the paper around the vase and secure the other vertical edge. The cut edges of the image should meet without any gap. The votive is ready for a candle.

TILE COASTERS

Reproduced on tiles with Lazertran Iron-on Transfer Paper, your pictures take on an instant patina that recalls vintage photos. Graphic, simple images work best and will look good even if the transfer isn't pristine. Buy extra tiles as it takes a while to get the timing down and you'll need some for weights. Once you get the hang of it, you'll be making sets for all your friends.

1 Sand the tiles to smooth away any roughness (pitting is okay). Wipe off any dust with a damp sponge and set the tiles aside to dry.

2 Using your image-editing software, size the images ⅛ inch smaller than the tiles. If the image contains type, remember to flip it before printing so it reads correctly on the finished tile. Do test prints on regular paper. Cut out these images and try different arrangements on the tiles to decide their final size and placement.

3 Print the images onto transfer paper, following the manufacturer's instructions. Cut out the images, leaving ⅛-inch plain borders.

4 **For the transfers:** Working with 1 tile at a time in an ovenproof pan, preheat the unglazed tile in a 350 degree oven for about 4 minutes until the tile is warm. Remove the pan from the oven and turn the oven up to 400 degrees. Place the transfer facedown on the warm tile; the transfer can smear while hot, so be very careful not to dislodge it. Place 5 or 6 plain tiles (or 1 tile and a brick) on top of the transfer in order to press it against the warm tile, and return the pan to the oven. After 2–4 minutes, carefully remove the weights (use those oven mitts!) and check the transfer. If the backing paper is curling or still looks white in spots, it hasn't completely adhered; replace the weights and leave it in the oven for another minute.

5 Allow the tile to cool until it is still warm but safe to handle, then remove the backing paper. Proceed very slowly or parts of the transfer might come off. (On the other hand, an incomplete transfer can produce interesting results.)

6 Once the tiles are completely cold, spray them with an acrylic spray coating to protect the transfer from smearing. Let them dry according to the manufacturer's directions, then brush on the Crystal Clear Glaze and allow to dry thoroughly. Affix cork or felt pads to the back of each tile.

IMAGES
Digital images at 150 dpi or higher (high resolution isn't critical)

COMPUTER TOOLS
Image-editing software
Inkjet printer

PANTRY CHECKLIST
Sponge
Scissors
Oven
Ovenproof pan or small cookie sheet
Oven mitts for handling tiles
Disposable paintbrush

MATERIALS
4- x 4-in. porous unglazed tiles (these can be ceramic, stone, or bisqueware)
Coarse sandpaper
Lazertran Iron-on Inkjet Transfer Paper (opaque or translucent)
1 brick (optional)
Acrylic spray coating
Krylon Triple-thick Crystal Clear Glaze
Self-adhesive cork or felt pads

▲15

►1

►2

"ANTIQUING" A NEW PHOTOGRAPH

IMAGES
Digital image at 300 or 350 dpi

COMPUTER TOOLS
Image-editing software

▶ **TIP** For those who use "grown-up" Photoshop, follow these 4 steps to convert a color image to black-and-white: Under MODE, convert your image to LAB COLOR. With the CHANNELS palette, throw away channels "a" and "b," then throw away channel "alpha 2." Change MODE to GRAYSCALE. Adjust LEVELS. ————

Here's how to digitally re-create the warm browns of the old sepia photographs that fill the pages of our cherished family albums. Our directions make it easy to produce images that look remarkably close to those heirloom portraits. First, you learn how to convert a color image to black-and-white with good tonal range of dense blacks, crisp whites, and many shades of gray. Then, we explain how to "age" your photo to a lovely soft brown tone. Adding a grainy visual texture to your artwork will add a further patina common to old-style photographic prints. That's the final technique.

1–2. TO CONVERT AN IMAGE FROM COLOR (RGB MODE) TO BLACK-AND-WHITE (GRAYSCALE MODE)

1 If the white areas of your photo have a pastel tint, improve the color balance of your RGB image by choosing ENHANCE/ADJUST COLOR/REMOVE COLOR CAST.

2 To remove all color from your photo, choose ENHANCE/ADJUST COLOR/REMOVE COLOR. You will now have a grayscale image.

3 Open the LEVELS (ENHANCE/ADJUST LIGHTING/LEVELS). You will see a graph that represents all the tones in your image; beneath it is a bar with three moveable triangles. The black curve of the graph should reach all the way to the ends of the bar. If it does not, move the left and right triangles toward the center until they are at the ends of the black curve. If the midtones of your image are too dark, move the center slider to the left until the image looks good to you (have PREVIEW checked so you can see the result). You should now have an image with dense black tones, crisp whites, and a wide range of grays in between.

4 Sharpen the image by choosing FILTER/SHARPEN/UNSHARP MASK and start with 60%.

5 Save your black-and-white image under a new name so you don't write over the original color version.

continued

3. TO MAKE A SEPIA-TONED IMAGE

① Start with a quality black-and-white version of your image, following the previous steps. You may not want to sharpen the image; many older images have an appealing softness that is worth replicating.

② Choose ENHANCE/ADJUST COLOR/COLOR VARIATIONS, then select MIDTONES. To give your image a sepia tint, click INCREASE RED, then click DECREASE BLUE. If you don't like the results, click RESET IMAGE, then move the AMOUNT slider, and again click INCREASE RED, then DECREASE BLUE.

③ If the blacks in the image seem too strong, select SHADOWS/LIGHTEN. You may need to repeat this step several times to get the result you want.

④ You can also soften the background, if you like. Select the background with the LASSO tool, give it a feather of 6 or 8 pixels (SELECT/FEATHER), and blur the background by choosing FILTER/BLUR/GAUSSIAN BLUR. The higher you set the radius, the more it will blur.

⑤ Save your sepia version under a new name so you don't write over the black-and-white version.

4. TO MAKE AN IMAGE GRAINY

① First, if your black-and-white or sepia-toned image has a border and you don't want it speckled, select just the photograph with the RECTANGULAR MARQUEE tool.

② Choose FILTER/NOISE/ADD NOISE, and start with 10%. Have PREVIEW checked so you can see the result; proceed with caution, as it's easy to overdo the effect.

③ When you like the result, save your grainy version under a new name so you don't write over the sepia version.

PLAY Unify snapshots whose colors might otherwise clash by transforming them into sepia images that can be hung as a group. This technique also softens boldly colored photos intended for display in a room with a more subtle palette. And it gives any image an instant vintage look. You can "antique" any photo, but it's most fun if friends and family are the subjects.

DECOUPAGE SUITCASE

COVER AN OLD SUIT-CASE WITH TRAVEL MEMENTOS TO GIVE IT THE LOOK OF ONE THAT'S SEEN THE GRAND TOUR. Then use it as a fun storage piece. Paper ephemera—from snapshots to ticket stubs to postcards to train schedules—will work. Ours celebrate a French sojourn with scenes of Paris and Provence. Use original photos from a 1-hour photo shop or digitized images printed on heavy white photo paper. Glue photos down with decoupage medium or a multipurpose sealer (use the sealer as a finish coat as well, applying several layers to the entire suitcase if it will get heavy use). Use white craft glue to attach heavier card stock or photos glued around curves, if necessary, and then finish with more medium.

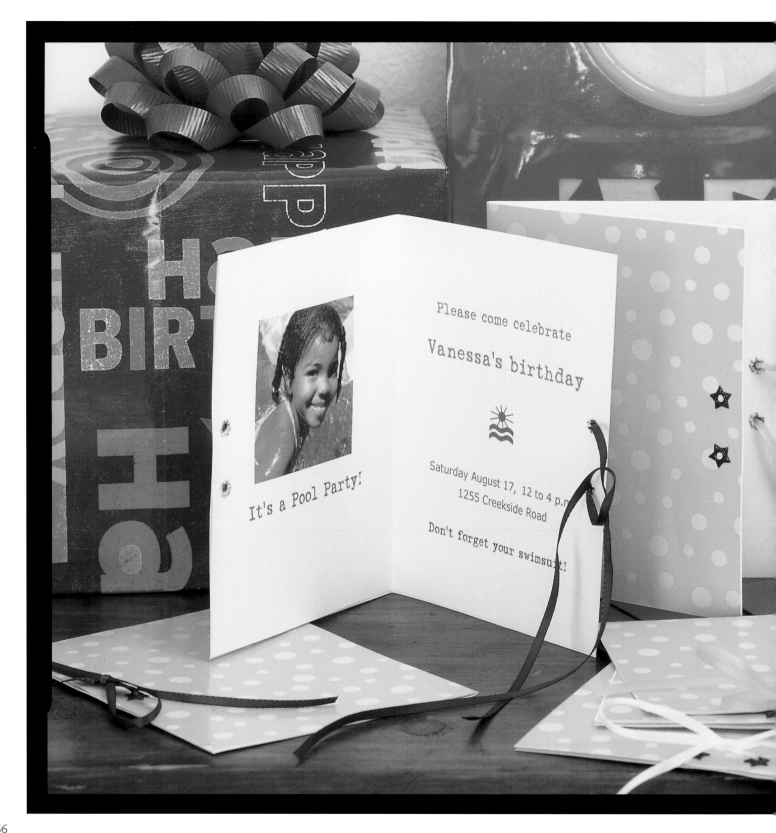

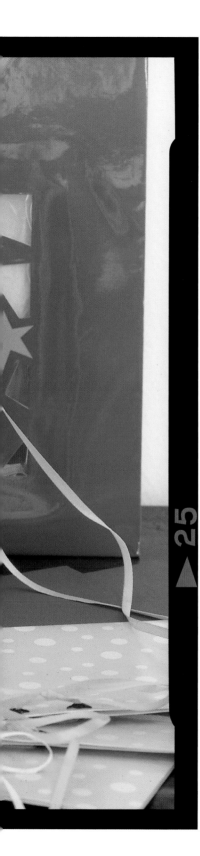

KIDS' PARTY INVITATIONS

Master a few simple image-editing techniques and you can create wonderful invitations at home that look truly professional. They're quick, easy, and depending on the paper, appropriate for any event, low-key or lavish. In fact, you'll spend far more time in an art supply store selecting papers than you will crafting a party's worth of invitations.

1 Open up the digital image you will want to appear on the interior of your card. Next, create a new document that is 8½ x 11 inches (landscape orientation), with a white background. Copy and paste your digital image onto the top left quadrant of the new document, 1 inch down from the top and 1 inch in from the left margin.

2 Click on the TYPE tool, and in the TYPE OPTIONS bar, select the font name, size, color, and alignment that you want for the invitation wording. Then click in the top right quadrant of your layout and type in the text, ending each line with a return. Any line can then be re-selected by double-clicking on it, and the color, size, and placement of wording adjusted. Keep all text at least ½ inch away from the center of the page (this will be the invitation fold) and from the right margin (so the eyelets won't punch holes through the text). When you are happy with your layout, choose LAYERS/FLATTEN IMAGE and save it.

continued

IMAGES
Digital image at 200 dpi or better

COMPUTER TOOLS
Image-editing software
Inkjet or laser printer

PANTRY CHECKLIST
Scissors
Craft knife or rotary cutter
Cutting mat
Metal ruler
Hammer

MATERIALS FOR 8 INVITATIONS
Cover: 4 sheets of 8½- x 11-in. paper
Insert: 4 sheets of 8½- x 11-in. paper
    (compatible with your printer)
⅛-in.-diameter hole punch
1 package ⅛-in. eyelets (you need
    4 per invitation)
Eyelet setter
4 yd. ⅛-in. ribbon, cut into 18-in.
    lengths
8 envelopes, size A6 (4¾ x 6½ in.)

Project Dimensions: Our cards are 4¼ x 5½ in. high once folded; the image is 2¼ in. square but it can be as large as the card if you prefer.

▶ **TIP** The paper for the interior message must be printable, a good backdrop for type, and complementary to the image (if your daughter insists on bright pink stock, be sure she understands that her face on the card will also be bright pink). White or pale colors always work and papers with little flecks can be fun. If you use a translucent stock like vellum, remember that any pattern or texture from the cover paper will show through. ———————————————

③ To print 2 invitations on a single sheet of 8½- x 11-inch paper, duplicate your layout as follows: Using the RECTANGULAR MARQUEE tool, select the top half of your page. Then, select the MOVE tool and hold down the OPTION key (Mac) or ALT key (Windows) until the pointer changes into a double arrow, then drag a copy of the layout to the bottom half of your page and release when it is aligned with the top layout. Save the file again.

④ Make a test print on plain paper, cut the sheet in half, then fold each part in half to confirm that the image and text are where they should be. (If they're not, tweak their positions and do another test print. Repeat until all the elements are exactly where you want them. This may take a few tries.) With the invitation folded, mark on the outside the position for 2 eyelets; punch holes through both layers at these marks. Save this sample as your template for the final invitations.

⑤ Print out the inserts on the actual paper. Using a craft knife or rotary cutter and cutting mat, cut both the cover paper and inserts into half sheets. Carefully fold each sheet, creasing well. For the cover, have the decorative side out; for the message page, have the text on the inside.

⑥ **To assemble each invitation:** Pair an insert (faceup) and cover (facedown), making sure edges are aligned. Using your template, mark on the front cover where the eyelets will go. Punch eyelet holes through all 4 layers at once (this is important!).

⑦ Open up the invitation, keeping the papers aligned. Set an eyelet into 1 hole, with its unfinished side on the inside of the invitation, and rest it on the cutting mat. Put the eyelet setter on the eyelet's unfinished side and tap it firmly 2 or 3 times with a hammer until it is flattened against the paper. Repeat with the remaining 3 holes and eyelets. Thread a length of ribbon through the eyelets and tie in a bow on the front of the invitation.

PLAY Here's a chance to work with those gorgeous papers that we all love but aren't printer-friendly. For the cover, which isn't printed, your choices range from fragile, shiny, handmade, or textured stock to rice paper embedded with leaves and flowers to foils or even wrapping paper. Use a unique paper for each invitation or have them all match.

HOLIDAY GIFT WRAP

IN JUST MINUTES WITH A COLOR PHOTOCOPIER, CONVERT SNAPSHOTS INTO PLAYFUL, PERSONAL WRAPPING PAPER. Any photo format works fine, but prints with white borders look framed, a nice touch. Be sure to arrange the images facedown on the copier glass, then fully cover with a sheet of colored paper. Avoid foil papers, as these will come out dark gray. Print on large-size paper such as ledger (11 x 17 inches) or poster (20 x 24 inches). For a matching card, glue a trimmed color-copy image to a metal-edged gift tag.

NOTE CARDS

THINKING OF YOU

Here is a card that is also a gift—the cover panel displays your hand-colored print of a favorite black-and-white photo (see Hand-Colored Photographs, page 86). The recipient will surely want to frame it, so secure the print to the card with removable mounting tape that lifts away easily and safely from the paper. This print brings back memories of a delightful, romantic trip taken by Laurie and her husband—before the boys enlarged their family! A scrap piece of rough-finish watercolor paper with a deckle edge makes a beautifully textured ground for the image, which is set off with a simple pencil line.

FATHER'S DAY

Make your wishes personal. Laura scanned an old snapshot of her with her dad, then attached it with eyelets (see Kids' Party Invitations, page 67) to a card that she made. To create the card, she mounted decorative wrapping paper on Bristol board then added a label that she hand-lettered with a greeting. Laura thought the theme of old postcards would please her dad, who collects stamps. He loved it.

FOR A BIG BIRTHDAY

A special birthday deserves a special card. To create the image, Laurie compiled strips of black-and-white snapshots taken of a friend (the birthday girl) over the years, glued the strips back-to-back, and assembled the strips so they spelled it all out. She took a digital photo of the collage and printed the copies on silver self-adhesive film for a festive look. (The film is easily cut and peeled off its backing paper after printing.) Use the prints as the cover for your cards, easily made from nice Bristol board or card stock.

NEW BABY

Get these ready before the baby arrives (while you have the time), then fill in the details after. The blue card is made from pre-printed vellum. The mini photo envelope is also vellum and is self-adhesive, but vellum tape would work fine. We tinted the photo to continue the blue theme (see "Antiquing" a New Photograph, page 63) and printed it on heavy photo paper—although even wallet-sized snaps from a 1-hour photo shop would be adorable. The name and birth information are on a separate card (not shown) inserted into slits on the inside of the main card. With your computer, prepare the announcement insert several to a page, print on nice paper stock, and cut apart. A very easy project for a parent-to-be.

...hat they called Sarah Ann.

FAMILY PHOTO ALBUM

IMAGES
20 digital images at 200 dpi or higher

COMPUTER TOOLS
Image-editing software
Inkjet or laser printer

PANTRY CHECKLIST
Craft knife
Cutting mat
Metal ruler
Pencil
Hole punch
Hammer
Rubber bands or binder clips

MATERIALS
21 sheets 8½- x 11-in. Epson Matte
    Heavyweight paper
1 sheet colored or handmade paper,
    for end sheets
1 sheet colored poster board, for the
    covers
Bone folder or blunt butter knife
Dritz Color Snap Tool
Dritz Color Snaps

Project Dimensions: The size of our
completed book is 7½ x 5½ in.

Those silly snapshots of your brother growing up can become a very personal and welcoming gift for your new sister-in-law when made into a small book complete with captions. Ours starts with baby pictures and ends with the engagement photo. The snapshots were scanned so they could be returned to the family album; this also lets you make them a uniform size and retouch cracks and dirt that have accumulated over the years.

1 Gather the photos you wish to include in the book; we used 20 total. Resize them to be 4 inches high (or 4 inches wide for landscape orientation) at 200 dpi. Print 1 copy of each on inexpensive paper and organize them into a sequence that you like. By hand, write a caption (such as names, dates, location, comments) below each image.

2 Using your image-editing software, create a master file. Create a new document that is 7½ inches wide x 5½ inches high at 200 dpi. (Finished pages will be 7 inches wide; the extra half-inch is to allow for the coil binding.) With RULERS showing, select the LINE tool and draw a 1-pixel-wide light gray line down the page at 4 inches (hold down the SHIFT key as you draw to keep the line straight). Draw a horizontal line that crosses this center line at 2¾ inches down from the top. On the LAYERS palette select FLATTEN IMAGE and save the new file as Page Master. (NOTE: If the rules disappear when you flatten, enlarging the window will make them reappear.)

3 For each page of the book, duplicate the Page Master file and save it as "Page 1," "Page 2," and so on. Open the first image to appear in the book and the document "Page 1" and copy and paste the image into the "Page 1" document. Using the MOVE tool, center the image on the intersecting lines (resize if necessary).

4 To add the caption, click on the TYPE tool and set the choices for your preferred font name, point size, and color. Click the box for centered alignment. Click with the TYPE tool right on the vertical line and about ¼ inch below the photo. Type in the caption you wrote for it on your preliminary layout (Step 1). Save the file again; DON'T flatten the layers.

5 Repeat Steps 3 and 4 to create pages 2 through 20, placing 1 photo and its caption per document. When complete, print out all 20 documents on inexpensive paper; be sure you

continued

► **TIP** Any copy shop that does spiral (coil) binding can finish the album for you in about 5 minutes for about $5. We suggest you have them trim it, too. While you can trim it yourself, it will take forever! It's also a challenge to line up the pages and cut them exactly square. ────────

check off PRINT CROP MARKS in the PRINT dialog box so you will know where to trim the book pages. Proofread all printed pages for typing mistakes and reconfirm that everything is to your liking.

6 You must remove the lines used as placement guides before you print out all pages on quality paper. Open the files 1 at a time, make sure you have chosen the background layer (it should be highlighted in blue), and draw a marquee to select the entire layout. Under EDIT, choose FILL/USE WHITE at 100% OPACITY. This will erase the lines. FLATTEN all files. (Once you do this, you will not be able to change the captions.)

7 Print out the final pages on the heavyweight stock. Have the pages trimmed at the crop marks at a copy shop (see Tip, left). At home, assemble the photos in your chosen sequence. For our book we also added a blank first page to write an inscription to the recipient. You may want to add a blank last page as well—a nice finish that also protects the final image page. Add an end sheet of colored or handmade paper, cut to page size, before the blank first page and after the last page.

8 **To make the covers:** Cut a 7½- x 5¾-inch piece of poster board for the front cover and a 9½- x 5¾-inch piece for the back cover. Score the inside of the back cover with a bone folder or blunt butter knife held against a ruler at 7½ inches and 7⅞ inches from the left edge. Carefully fold along the score lines.

9 On the flap of the back cover, mark where the snaps will go, about ¾ inch from the side edge and 1¼ inches in from top and bottom edges. Punch a hole through each of these marks. Line up the front and back covers (see diagram, left) with flap folded over the right end; on the front cover, make a pencil mark through the 2 punched holes. Punch holes at these 2 marks as well. Install snaps through all 4 holes according to the manufacturer's instructions. Be sure the snap sockets are on the outside of the front cover and the studs on the inside of the back cover.

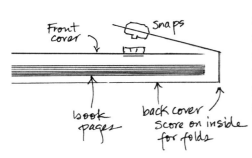

10 Fasten the snaps, place the book pages between the covers, and check for alignment. If necessary, trim the cover slightly to make it square. Reconfirm that the pages are in the correct order and secure the book, pages and covers, with rubber bands or binder clips. At a copy shop, have the book finished with a coil binding on its left edge.

YOUR OWN BRAND

USE SELF-ADHESIVE PAPER AND YOUR PRINTER (OR A PHOTOCOPIER) TO CREATE PERSONAL STATIONERY, BUSINESS CARDS, AND PACKAGING for your hobby, home business, household or just for you. To make labels for her "I wish-I-really-*had*-canned-it-at-home" blueberry jam business, Caroline chose a picture of a blueberry on a plain surface (most jam labels look old-fashioned and fussy; she wanted hers to be simple and fresh). Using image-editing software, she cropped the image, added her logo and type, and printed out labels of varying sizes on 8½- x 11-inch self-adhesive paper. The simple image lends itself to all sorts of variations: resize it (by computer, color copier, or with scissors in hand), change the colors and backgrounds, or zoom in on details. Find complementary paper, envelopes, cards, etc., at your local stationer or art supply store. You're in business!

Height _____ In. 75-0   Head Leng[...]

Eng. Height _____ 5 8 7/8   Head Width

Outside A _____ In. 75-0   Cheek Width

Trunk _____ 91.3   R. Ear

Remarks Incident)
to Measurement) _____

MITCH'S ACCORDION FRAME

MITCH'S ACCORDION FRAME

IMAGES
3 images of equal size

PANTRY CHECKLIST
Metal ruler

MATERIALS
6 panels of ⅛-in.-thick sheet acrylic
    plastic (like Plexiglas), cut and
    drilled to your specifications
12 screws (long enough to fit through
    2 layers of the acrylic plastic)
12 wing nuts, to fit screws
24 steel washers, to fit screws
Spool of copper or steel wire (picture
    wire is fine), 20–25 gauge (the
    higher the gauge, the thinner the
    wire)
Wire cutters

Project Dimensions: Our prints
measure 5½ in. wide x 6 in. high; the
margins are 1 inch all around; the panels
are 7½ in. wide by 8 in. high.

An ingenious and very cheap framing solution that works at any size. Here we show you how to make a hinged tabletop accordion frame with three panels, but the same technique can easily be adapted to a single photograph (without the hinges) or expanded to include several more panels. Choose wing nuts, screws, washers, and wire that most appeal to you, as they are used for decoration as well as to join the panels.

① Determine the size of your acrylic panels by adding a minimum of 1 inch to the dimensions of your prints.

② Bring a set of prints and hardware with you when you have your acrylic panels cut to size. At the plastics dealer or framer, ask the clerk to: (a) cut 3 pairs of equal-size panels per your dimensions (it is crucial that each pair is perfectly aligned when stacked), (b) mark the placement of the screw holes (they should not be less than ¾ inch from each corner), (c) double-check the alignment of each stacked pair, (d) drill holes through each stack that are the right size for your hardware.

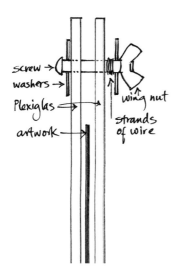

screw →
washers →
Plexiglas →
artwork →
wing nut
strands of wire

③ **To assemble the panels:** Position your pictures evenly between each pair of acrylic plastic panels. Be sure the holes line up. Thread your screws, wing nuts, and washers in place, but don't tighten them yet. (In our example, Mitch has alternated the wing nuts so some face front and some face back. This is fine as long as the frame sits on a table. If you plan to hang it, be sure the wing nuts all face front and that the screws protrude evenly from the back, so the frame doesn't wobble against the wall.)

④ To create the wire border, wrap the wire around the 4 corner screws of each panel and under the washers as many times as you like to achieve your desired effect (see diagram, left). Snip the wire free with wire cutters and tie off the end under one of the washers. Don't tighten the wing nuts yet!

⑤ To create the accordion's hinges, lay your panels on a table ¼ inch apart, with tops and bottoms lined up (you can butt them against a metal ruler to be sure they're flush). Wrap the wire several times around the side-to-side wing nuts on neighboring panels. Snip and tie off the wire. Now you can tighten the wing nuts!

▶ **TIP** As the frame is open on all sides and does not use a mat, it is not technically archival. If this concerns you, scan your images at 300 dpi, print them on gorgeous paper, and tuck your originals away. ———

PLAY If you want to frame a single wall-sized image, ask for advice about the thickness of the acrylic plastic before you have it cut; if it's too thin it will bow when hung. To hang a larger piece, wrap the wire multiple times around the top 2 screws before tightening the wing nuts; the heavier the piece, the more wire you'll need. Be sure to test it first. Hang your frame from a nail that you've glued a wing nut to so the "hanger" feels like an extension of the piece.

PET PLACE MATS

Even the most winsome pooch or kitty creates a mess around the food and water bowls. Turned off by the "cutesy" pet mats she could buy, Laura created ones she could live with. Anyone who has pets they adore will love these mats as gifts (plus, if they have a really big dog, you can make them a really BIG mat). They're kid-proof, too! Make mats for humans with the same technique and any imagery. Use a service bureau to enlarge and print the image on canvas.

1 Either at home or at a service bureau, size and crop your digital images so they can be printed at 100% of the final size of the mat. At a service bureau, have the images printed with an inkjet printer on white roll canvas, leaving a margin of blank canvas around the image (helpful when you laminate it later on).

2 Protect your work surface with the kitchen towel. Preheat the iron to a medium setting (no steam). Set your printed canvas, faceup, on the towel. Cut the sheet of iron-on vinyl in half, peel off the paper backing from one half, and place the vinyl, sticky side down, over your image. Smooth in place with your hands.

continued

IMAGES
Digital images, enlarged to your desired
  size at minimum 100 dpi

COMPUTER TOOLS
Image-editing software

PANTRY CHECKLIST
Smooth kitchen towel
Household iron
Scissors
Small bowl, for shaping the template
Pencil
Transparent tape
White craft glue

MATERIALS
Iron-on vinyl, 17 in. wide
  Large mat (dog) requires 4 ft.
  Small mat (cat) requires 2½ ft.
Scrap cardboard
Black ½-in.-wide polyester foldover
  binding (enough for the entire
  perimeter of the mat plus some
  overlap)
1 roll ½-in.-wide double-face fusible
  web (sold in fabric stores)

Project Dimensions: Our large mat (dog) is 15 x 20 in.; the small mat (cat) is 12 x 16 in. Both are 200 dpi, enlarged from fairly high resolution digital photos.

3 Iron the vinyl to set it, following the manufacturer's instructions. The vinyl is adhered when it loses its sheen and the weave pattern of the canvas begins to show through. Flip the mat and repeat the process on the plain back side (less ironing time will be needed).

4 Trim off the blank canvas margins. Make a rounded corner template from scrap cardboard, using a small bowl to form a curve. Trace the template with a pencil on the vinyl at each corner; trim the corners.

5 Cut a length of binding that goes completely around the perimeter of the mat with some extra for overlap. To prevent frayed ends while you work, place a piece of tape on the inside of each end of the binding, then trim the binding in the middle of the tape.

6 To secure the binding to the mat, you will attach it to the front (image) side first and then attach the back side. Cut 1-foot lengths of fusible web and press its sticky side on the inside of the binding along one side only (be sure it doesn't show on the outside). Overlap the pieces as you work along the binding. Once you get all the way around, peel away the backing paper.

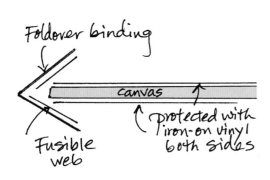

Foldover binding

Fusible web

canvas

protected with iron-on vinyl both sides

7 Set the place mat image side up. To secure the binding to the mat, starting in the middle of 1 straight side, fit the binding over the edges of the mat and press it in place with your fingers, see diagram, left (the adhesive on the fusible web will hold it as you work around the mat). Do all the straight sides first, then the corners, easing in the fullness as you press down.

8 Where the ends of the binding overlap, retape the binding on the inside (per Step 5) and trim so the ends of the binding just meet. Place a little more fusible web under the taped areas and secure. Iron the edging in place, protecting the mat with paper as you did when ironing the vinyl or with an ironing cloth. Iron just the binding, as the vinyl will soften again with heat.

9 Repeat Steps 6–8 to attach the binding to the back side of the mat, but stick the strips of fusible web onto the vinyl (not the binding) for the straight sides. For the corners, trim the web strips a little narrower and place them on the binding. Remove their backing paper, press down, then iron as before. Secure the binding ends from fraying with a dab of glue; smooth any loose ends into the glue and let dry.

PLAY Here's a simpler version that goes together in a flash, as you eliminate the binding. Just trim the mat to final size before you iron on the vinyl (cut the vinyl larger than the canvas to create fusible edges), then heat-fuse the edges of the vinyl with your iron until they are sealed.

IT'S EASY TO ADAPT THIS TECHNIQUE to smaller projects like a baby's bib. Use snapshots downloaded from an online photo album or recent e-mail. An existing bib can be traced as a pattern. A gift of one or two of them would please any new parents.

YOUR OWN ANDY WARHOL

Capture your inner celebrity. An Andy Warhol portrait was once solely for the rich and famous. But we'll show you how easy it is to replicate the look of a Warhol without the sticker shock of an original. It's a photographic sleight of hand, using the SELECTION tools and PAINT BUCKET features of your image-editing software. As a gift, it will dazzle anyone—from a bride and groom to teenagers who think they've seen it all. Laurie made this one to give to her nephew, pictured here with her son.

> ▶ **TIP** Selecting specific areas of your image can be done with a variety of tools in your image-editing software. Once you become familiar with the range of selection tools, you'll have a good sense as to which works best for any particular image. The MAGIC WAND tool is useful for selecting areas with similar color, while you might try the SELECTION BRUSH or MAGNETIC LASSO (which clings to edges of a shape) to select a more complex area, such as a figure in a landscape. Often you will want to use more than one tool to refine your selection. Spend some time experimenting with these tools. You'll notice the difference in everything you do.

① Open your digital image in your image-editing software.

② Use the THRESHOLD command (under FILTER/ADJUSTMENTS) to convert your picture into a high-contrast black-and-white image. Move the slider until you get a good balance between black outlines and white space.

③ Using the MAGNETIC LASSO (and/or other selection tools), outline the subject of your image, separating it from its background. Once you have the subject area selected, COPY and PASTE it. You have created a new layer with just the subject (the area you selected) on it. Now the image has 2 layers: the background and the subject layer.

NOTE: You may find it easier to outline your subject and cut and paste it onto its own layer *before* you make the threshold adjustments. If so, you will need to perform the threshold adjustment on both the subject and background layers separately.

④ Select the background layer. Then select the color you'd like for the background. Fill in the white spaces in the background by clicking on those areas with the PAINT BUCKET tool.

⑤ Select the subject layer. Select a different color for the subject and, again, using PAINT BUCKET, fill in the white spaces. Use different colors in different areas as you like and continue to fill in all the white space until the image is complete. Save your image as a TIFF file.

NOTE: If a white area isn't completely surrounded by black, PAINT BUCKET will spread the color into surrounding shapes. To resolve this, use LASSO or MAGNETIC LASSO to select and isolate a particular area of the image, then copy and paste that selection onto another layer. Click on that layer and use PAINT BUCKET to fill in just that layer.

⑥ **To create 4 different versions of the image:** Duplicate your image. Repeat Steps 4–7 with different colors, then FLATTEN your image. Do this two more times until you have 4 different versions of the image.

⑦ Create a new document that is 8½ x 11 inches (landscape orientation), or whatever is twice the width and twice the height of one of your images. Make sure the resolution of the new document matches that of your digital images.

⑧ Copy and paste each of the 4 files into this new document. Use the MOVE tool to place each one in position and save this new document.

⑨ Print out the image and frame it.

HAND-COLORED PHOTOGRAPHS

IMAGES

Black-and-white image, printed in the darkroom on matte photo paper (5- x 7-in. or 8- x 10-in. prints work well)

MATERIALS

Freezer paper
Masking tape, optional
Marshall's Photo Oils (available in sets of 5 or more colors)
Cotton-tip cosmetic applicators with flat ends
Small 100% cotton cosmetic pads

▶ **TIP** This technique uses oil paints that only work on matte photo paper. Color images—what most of us shoot today—can be converted to black-and-white (see "Antiquing" a New Photograph, page 63) and then sent to a photo lab to be printed in the traditional manner on photo paper. ——

Before the invention of color printing, black-and-white photos were colorized by hand. While modern printers have rendered hand-tinting obsolete, it's a lost art well worth exploring for the beauty of the finished image. You'll achieve the most satisfactory results from simple subjects without much fussy detail, like Laurie's photograph of doorways in Tuscany that Laura hand colored. Faces are fairly challenging. Landscapes, scenery, or flowers work beautifully, as colors blend one tone into another. Success requires a little patience and some practice, but the reward is a work of art that replicates the patina of antique prints. A computer just can't get you there.

NOTE: Making this project is totally dependent on the image you use, and the technique is thoroughly explained in the directions that accompany the oil paints. So, instead of the usual step-by-step instructions used elsewhere in the book, here are helpful guidelines and tips from Laura, based on what works for her when hand-coloring images. Read them over carefully before you begin.

● Cover your work surface well with freezer paper, taping it in place if necessary. The paper will both protect the surface and serve as a disposable palette to mix the oils.

● The gist of this technique is to apply a lot of color and remove most of it until you achieve a shade you like. The paint dries quite slowly; it's very easy to remove color up until it dries (even then, you can use the solvent supplied with the oils to lift it off).

● As the oils are transparent, pale colors are created by applying very thin layers of color over white paper, which shows through and lightens the color to a pale shade. Images with lots of light areas are easy to tint in almost any color. Gray areas will look fine if tinted with earth tones or darker colors, but will muddy and darken colors like yellow, light green, and pink.

● As a first step, select the dominant colors for the large areas (we colored the three buildings salmon red, green, and yellow ochre). If it's a landscape, start with the sky.

● Apply color to an area with a cotton pad right over the details in the image. Then carefully remove colors in areas that you want to lighten. Use cotton pads to lighten large areas and cosmetic applicators to remove color from fine detail.

continued

No color in real life is one perfectly flat tone, but rather is composed of varying shades of a color with other tones mixed in. For the yellow house we added dark ochre and rust brown to the shadow areas, blending them in with cotton applicators. The green house was too glaringly green, so we lightened the open areas of the walls by removing more color, and added blue tints to the shadows.

Use Neutral Tint (a thin gray color) to further vary the depth and strength of shadows to give the image more dimension. Combine it with warm tones to create shadows in warm-hued areas, or use it full strength to darken cooler areas. Let your photograph guide you as to which areas should appear darker. Create or deepen blacks in an image by applying a thin layer of black oil paint.

The only color in your paint set that is truly opaque is White. Use it sparingly, as it draws the eye. (We lightened the curtains and trim of the upstairs window with white.) Besides standing out, white takes forever to dry—up to 5 days—so be sure to apply it last. But it creates needed highlights better than anything else.

Work slowly, adding small amounts of color at a time. Step back once in a while to study the effect. Don't worry about "brush" lines. No one will notice such fine detail from a viewing distance, just the overall effect. Eventually, the applied color marries with the photo beneath to create a remarkable work of art.

Allow several days for your image to dry (seriously!). Then, display it in your most elegant frame, or use it as cover art for a very special note card (see Thinking of You, page 70).

PLAY Don't feel that you must slavishly reproduce nature. Play around with color. If you don't like what you see, here's your opportunity to develop a palette more to your liking. Every painting is unique. That's part of the fun.

MIRROR FRAME

AN EXQUISITE GIFT FOR YOUR SPECIAL SWEETIE CAN BE MADE IN AN HOUR from a favorite frame and a piece of mirrored glass cut to fit it. With a single-edge razor blade clipped into a holder to protect fingers, we scraped away some of the mirror's black backing to create a "window" of clear glass for a photo to show through. It will take some work to completely remove the mirror coating but the results are worth the effort. The clear area can be large or small; square, oval, or heart shape; rough on the edges or neat and angular—you decide. Then simply tape your print to the back of the glass and reinstall it in the frame. A hand mirror or an antique mirror of any size will work as long as you can access its back. Mirrored glass can be purchased at stores that sell window glass.

CHAIR RAIL BORDER

IMAGES
Multiple digital images, sized to the same height, printed at 200 dpi

COMPUTER TOOLS
Image-editing software
Inkjet printer

PANTRY CHECKLIST
Scissors or rotary cutter
Cutting mat
Metal ruler
Pencil
Foam roller, optional

MATERIALS
8½- x 11-in. self-adhesive paper
Cloth bookbinding tape or white masking tape (see Step 2 to determine
amount)
Water-resistant sealer

More fun than wallpaper! For yourself or to install as a gift, this easy border will brighten any room, from bathroom to nursery to den to bedroom. It's a perfect little weekend project when you're itching to transform a space with a small detail, rather than a total makeover. The images are photocopied onto self-adhesive paper, stuck on the wall, and finished with binding tape. How simple is that?

1 Choose pictures with a unifying theme or palette, like Caroline's water and beach shots in shades of blue, sepia, and sand. If you are trying to line up horizons as she did, you may need to adjust the size of certain images with your software.

2 Measure the length of the chair rail to determine the number and size of the images and the amount of binding tape you will need. Prepare the wall—sanding and painting it, if necessary. Ideally, it should be very smooth, or at least very clean.

3 Decide how high you'd like the chair rail border to be. Open the images you are going to use in your image-editing software and resize each one so that they are all the same height (the width of the images can vary). Keep in mind that the binding tape will cover at least $1/16$ inch of the upper and lower edges of each image, so allow room for that. For best results, make sure the images line up nicely as a border.

4 Print your images onto the self-adhesive paper. You can cut and paste 2 or 3 images into an 8½- x 11-inch document to print multiples on a sheet (three 4- x 6-inch images will fit on 1 sheet).

5 Cut out the images and place them so they form 1 long strip when you lay them out side by side.

6 Decide the width of the binding tape; if you want it narrower, cut it to size along the gridlines on the paper backing. Cut 2 long tape strips the length of the border. Don't remove their backing paper.

continued

▶ **TIP** This project can be done without the help of a computer, using a color copier at a copy shop or service bureau, provided you test your sealer first to be sure it doesn't smear the printouts. ———

7 Organize the photos as you like, and number them in this order on their back sides. Position (but don't adhere) 1 tape strip along the wall flush with the chair rail; using a ruler, draw a pencil line along the upper edge of the tape, creating a guide for picture placement.

8 Starting with photo 1, peel and stick the images in order onto the wall, placing their lower edges just below the pencil line. They can overlap slightly, but the fewer bumps, the better. When you are sure of their placement, press them firmly to smooth out any bubbles using your hands or a roller.

9 Coat the images with a water-resistant sealer according to the manufacturer's instructions and let dry.

10 To finish, peel off the backing from 1 strip of tape. Position it along the bottom of the border, overlapping the edge by $1/16$ inch. Press firmly to adhere. Repeat with the second tape strip along the top. Add vertical strips around windows and doors as needed.

⚠ CAUTION: Avoid using any smelly coating in a nursery or young child's room.

▶ **TIP** If mounted on a bathroom wall, it's wise to protect the border with a water-resistant sealer. Elsewhere, waterproofing isn't necessary, but it's a good idea to apply a coating with UV protection so the images don't fade. ————————

METAL TINS   HERE'S GIFT PACKAGING THAT'S A

GIFT IN ITSELF. These are plain tins purchased at any craft, art supply, or organizing store (or found at flea markets), embellished with photographs printed on self-adhesive paper. Choose a color or black-and-white digital image that has special meaning to the recipient or hints at what's inside. Your image can wrap fully around the tin (panoramic shots work best) or partway, like a label, or just cover the lid. Size the image a little larger than you'll need. Print, crop to fit, then apply. Filled with spices and teas, jewelry, beach stones, or other mementos, these tins will be treasured long after their contents are gone.

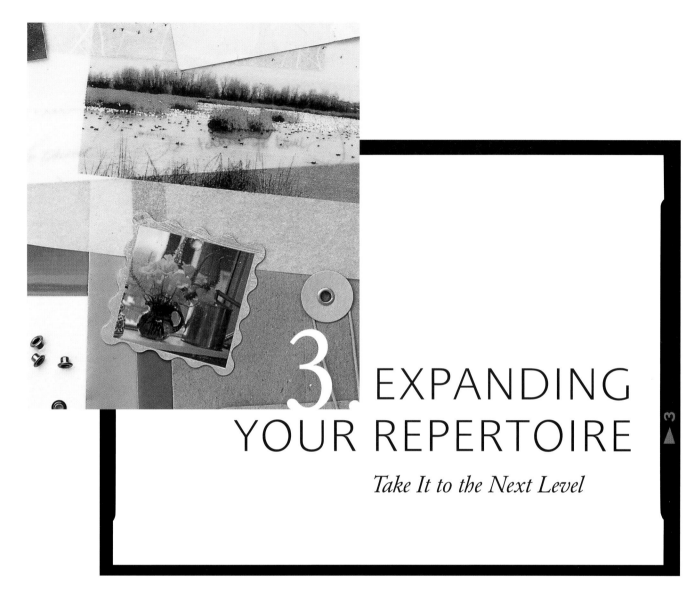

3. EXPANDING YOUR REPERTOIRE

Take It to the Next Level

BLUEPRINTS

These striking images are technically known as cyanotypes (cyan is a shade of blue used as one of the primary colors in printing). They're so easy to make even kids will get great results. You create the "negative" on a laser printer or copier (not an inkjet printer) and expose it in sunlight. Getting exactly the exposure you want can be tricky, but all sorts of interesting variations will happen in the meantime that you may love even more. Any subject matter works, but remember that everything and everyone will be blue. Choose images that are fairly high contrast—lots of black and white. If you need to heighten the contrast of a favorite photo, use the LEVELS or BRIGHTNESS/CONTRAST tool in your software.

IMAGES
Black-and-white digital images at
    300 dpi (see Step 1)

COMPUTER TOOLS
Laser printer or photocopier

PANTRY CHECKLIST
Freezer paper
Masking tape
Newspapers
Apron
Rubber gloves
3-in. natural-bristle brush
    continued

A FEW POINTERS: The smoother the paper, the finer the detail in the finished image. Do not mix more chemicals than you will use at a time or coat more paper than you can expose in one day, as the solution becomes unusable overnight. Be sure to use a sheet of acrylic plastic in Step 4, not glass. The latter absorbs ultraviolet light, the part of sunlight the chemicals are sensitive to, and that will dramatically change your results. A closet, storeroom, or window-less space where you can coat paper and let it dry in very low light can double as a darkroom.

1   If your images are in color, convert them to high-quality black-and-whites (see "Antiquing" a New Photograph, page 63), increasing the contrast if necessary. Print each on transparency film; the final size of the printed negative will be the final size of your blueprint image. If you want an image that prints as it was photographed, you will need to make it into a negative image before printing (FILTER/ADJUSTMENTS/INVERT).

2   Cover the plywood board with freezer paper and tape it down. Carefully tape 2 or 3 pieces of watercolor paper to the board at their corners. Before mixing the chemicals, protect your work surface with newspaper and yourself with an apron and rubber gloves. In your designated darkroom space, assemble the plywood board, brush, bowl, measuring cup, paper towels, and photographic chemicals.

continued

PANTRY CHECKLIST, continued
Small glass bowl
Glass measuring cup
Paper towels
Hair dryer, optional
Large binder clips or clamps
Timer
Scissors

MATERIALS

8½- x 11-in. transparency film
Scrap plywood board large enough to
    hold 2 or 3 sheets of watercolor
    paper
8- x 10-in. sheets of heavyweight water-
    color paper (140 lb. or heavier)
Cyanotype Kit (from Photographer's
    Formulary)
⅛-in.-thick sheet acrylic plastic (like
    Plexiglas), the same size as the
    plywood board

Project Dimensions: Our negatives and
images are 5 x 7 in.

3   To coat the watercolor paper, mix equal parts of the chemicals with the brush in the glass bowl to make about ¼ cup (mix small batches at a time, as the chemicals lose potency after a few hours). Brush the solution on the paper as evenly as possible, applying it first up and down, then side to side. As your visibility is limited in the dark work area, the more methodical you can be, the more even the coat. Absorb any puddles around the edges of the paper with paper towels. Rinse the brush. Let the paper dry completely on the board and in the dark (a hair dryer will speed the process). Heavily textured paper will require a second coat to ensure that the solution covers it completely; let the paper dry between coats.

4   **To make the exposures:** Place a negative on each sheet of coated paper. Cover all with the acrylic plastic sheet and clip or clamp it to the board. Place the board in sunlight. At first the paper will be bright yellow green, then turn blue green, then finally, gray or olive gray. Start with a test exposure of 10–12 minutes if it's a bright, sunny day. Exposure time will vary depending on time of day, the season, the latitude, the paper used, and the particular negative. You may need to experiment with exposure times to find the one that is right for your location and materials.

5   When time is up, remove the prints from the board and rinse them under running water for 5 minutes to remove all coating chemicals. The print will turn blue in the water and the image will emerge. Keep rinsing until details show in shadow areas and the yellow has washed off the highlights. (Overwashing will lighten the blue areas.) The print will look teal blue at this point; it deepens to indigo and increases in contrast as it dries. Hang prints or lay them flat on a baker's cooling rack to dry.

6   When done for the day, discard all solution and wash out everything well; run the bowl and cup through the dishwasher before returning them to the pantry.

PLAY   Instead of making a negative with a photograph, use a drawing rendered on clear acetate instead. Try black or red marking pen, India ink, whiteout, or black oil pastel. Shadings in pencil may or may not come out well. Cut paper or cellophane into graphic shapes to make designs. Opaque materials will block light and appear as blank spots; transparent and translucent materials will make areas of tone. To add handwriting to the photograph, write with one of the above tools on clear film and expose it along with the negative.

JEWEL CASE DISPLAY

DON'T THROW OUT UNWANTED CD CASES. REUSE THEM FOR AN INEXPENSIVE PHOTO GALLERY, as Laura did here. Create a display for yourself or send one of favorite faces and places to cheer a faraway friend or lonely grandparents. Scan and crop your images to the size of the case (5⅜ x 4⅝ inches high), then print on good photo paper and trim. Use standard (not slim) cases, old or newly purchased at office supply or music stores. Discard their plastic inserts. Back each photo with cardboard or foamboard and snap the cases shut. Attach them to the wall with 3-inch strips of sticky-back hook-and-loop fasteners (such as Velcro). Now you can change your art as easily as you change your mind!

SILK SCARF

Laura calls it a scarf, but we say it's a walking photo gallery and beautiful work of art that will inspire admiring glances wherever you (or lucky recipients) wear it. Abstracts are a good choice for the images, as are landscapes, garden details, travel photos—anything but people. Be sure to choose a fabric that drapes well, isn't so thin that it is a challenge to sew, and doesn't ravel. Medium-weight silks like Habotai are your best bet. Laura used the same silk front and back for hers, but obviously they can differ.

1 With your image-editing software, size and crop your images so that the image fills an area at least 8¼ x 10¼ inches. Print the images on the silk fabric sheets. (To avoid jams, we recommend that you first flatten the sheets as much as possible, then hand feed them 1 at a time through your printer.)

2 Let the printed images dry 24 hours, then peel and discard their paper backings. If you will be washing your scarf, hand wash your printed fabric squares now, following the manufacturer's instructions.

3 Cut 2 squares, each measuring 9 x 11 inches, from the lightweight white silk. Pin 1 square to the back of each image. Sew them together in the margins using a basting stitch.

4 Cut 2 panels from your medium-weight silk. For the front: 11 inches wide x 45 inches long. For the back: 11 inches wide x 61 inches long. Pin a printed image to either end of the front panel, right sides together. Sew them together with ½-inch seams; press seams open.

5 Pin the ribbon trim to the fabric where desired and top-stitch it onto the silk with matching thread. Trim ribbon ends flush with the edges of the silk. Press with a cool iron.

6 Pin the back and front panels down their long sides, right sides together; leave the narrow ends open. Sew the panels together with ½-inch side seams. Start at the same end of the scarf for both sides or the fabric will pull out of alignment. Check that that white margins of the images have been caught fully in the seams so they don't show on the front of the scarf.

continued

IMAGES
2 digital images measuring 10 in. wide x 8 in. high at 200 dpi minimum

COMPUTER TOOLS
Image-editing software
Inkjet printer

PANTRY CHECKLIST
Sharp scissors
Measuring tape or metal ruler
Straight pins
Sewing machine fitted with a fine needle (or needle and thread if hand-sewn)
Household iron
Sewing needle, to slip-stitch ends closed

MATERIALS
8½- x 11-in. silk fabric sheets
½ yd. lightweight white silk
2 yd. medium-weight silk, patterned or plain
Matching thread, for the main fabric
1 yd. accent ribbon, cut in half (not too stiff or it won't drape well)
Matching thread, for the ribbon, optional
4 tassels or ¼ yd. bead fringe

Project Dimensions: Our finished scarf measures 10 x 60 in. long, with image panels that are each 10 x 8 in. high.

▶ **TIP** You might want to wait to buy fabric, accent ribbon, and trim until after your images are printed. Laura found that her images were darker on the computer than on the silk fabric sheets, sending her off to the store to replace her original silk with one better suited to lighter values.

7 Turn the scarf inside out and press carefully. At each open end, turn under ½ inch of the front and back panels and press flat (the seam allowance will be inside the scarf). Turn the scarf right side out.

8 Tack 1 tassel or 3 strands of bead fringe in place at each corner of the scarf, fastening the trim well to the ½-inch seam allowance. Pin the ends of the scarf together and close them with a hand-sewn slip-stitch.

PLAY The entire length of the scarf can be images seamed together for a very dramatic and graphic result. However, be aware that the scarf will be bulkier and less fluid with each additional seam.

PAINTING WITH
PHOTO INSET

YOUR OWN PAINTING MAKES A UNIQUE BACK-DROP FOR A SPECIAL PHOTOGRAPH. It's also a fun experience for anyone, kid or grown-up, who likes to experiment with art materials. Have ready an image, a stretched white canvas in any size, brushes, acrylic or oil paints, and the appropriate varnish. Play with the paints on the canvas, trying different textures and colors. Here, Laurie layered only two colors, overlapping thick and thin coats. When you like the effect, coat it with varnish and let it dry briefly. While it's still tacky, position the photograph on the canvas. Apply several more coats of varnish, which both protects and "ages" the image, letting one dry before applying the next. If you prefer a clean image, varnish only the painting and the edges of the photo.

FAUX TINTYPE JEWELRY

Portrait miniatures of loved ones—this is Anne Jane Grant, Laura's great-great aunt—are part jewelry, part wearable family album. We digitized an heirloom photo, then transferred the image to metal, giving it the burnished look of a vintage tintype. Our necklace would be a very personal, one-of-a-kind gift for anyone you care about. You can purchase metal tags at craft stores or online, and the split rings, bail, and chain at beading or craft stores.

IMAGES
Digital image at 300 dpi

COMPUTER TOOLS
Image-editing software
Inkjet printer

PANTRY CHECKLIST
Waxed or freezer paper
¼-in. nylon-bristle brush
Rotary cutter
Cutting mat
Metal ruler
Clamp or binder clip
Small foam roller
Needle-nose pliers
White craft glue

MATERIALS
Heavyweight glossy white photo paper
1 bottle (8 oz.) Omni-Gel
8½- x 11-in. sheet thin black card stock
Rectangular Stitched Tin Tiles or metal tags
Large embroidery needle
1 skein (2 m) .5mm (#3) prethreaded black silk bead cord
2 silver split rings (8mm), to attach photo tile to bail
1 silver bail with large eye, for chain
18-in. silver chain with clasp that fits through the eye of the bail

1   With your image-editing software, size and crop your digital image so it fits within the punched holes that border the tin tile; print it out on photo paper. (It's easiest to print many different images on 1 sheet, with spares of each in case any get damaged in handling.)

2   Work on a smooth, clean surface like a laminate counter, plastic tablecloth, or plastic tray, protected with waxed or freezer paper. To prepare the image, set the print faceup on the work surface. Brush on a thin, even coat of Omni-Gel, using up-and-down strokes. Let dry. Apply a second coat, using side-to-side strokes. Let dry. Apply a final coat, brushing diagonally (corner to corner). Let dry thoroughly.

3   While the image is drying, cut a piece of the card stock with the rotary cutter and ruler to the exact size of a tin tile; clamp them together. With the embroidery needle, punch holes in the card stock following the punched pattern on the tile; set aside.

4   Cut out the image you will use, leaving a ¼-inch paper border around the photo for easy handling. Soak the image, glossy side up, in warm water for a few minutes, until the paper is completely wet.

5   Transfer the wet paper from the water to the work surface, setting it image side down. Smooth it so it makes full contact with the surface, lift off a corner with your fingernail, and then very, very gently peel away the paper from the back of the image. What will be left behind is a very thin, transparent film with the image sealed inside it.

6   Let this thin film dry on the work surface, making sure it's perfectly flat and squared up. When completely dry, peel it off the surface. At this point, trim away the paper margin using a rotary cutter and cutting mat. The remaining image should just fit within the border of holes on your tin tile.

continued

TIP Make this project when you're relaxed and someone else is answering the phone or putting the kids to bed. Give it your full attention and you'll have perfect results. ——

7 To mount the image, brush a thin layer of Omni-Gel on the tin tile and also on the back of the image; carefully set the image on the tile, patting it in place with your fingers. Using the foam roller, give it a final smoothing to eliminate air bubbles (if any air bubbles remain, use a needle to prick them in their centers and use your fingers to ease out any near the edges). Be very gentle; the image is still easily distorted. Small air bubbles should disappear when the image is completely dry. Let it dry overnight or until the background looks transparent, not white.

8 For best protection, apply 2 more thin coats of Omni-Gel, letting the image dry between coats.

9 **To assemble the pendant:** Place the black card stock on the back of the tin tile, aligning holes. Thread 1 split ring through each of the 2 top center holes of both (needle-nose pliers help).

10 Using the prethreaded bead cord, sew through the remaining holes: Start at the top edge, third hole from the right, and work clockwise (skip the split rings). Knot the cord in the back and glue down ends with a dab of craft glue.

11 Thread the small loop of the bail through both split rings and use the pliers to close the split rings. Thread the chain through the loop in the bail.

NOTE If Stitched Tin Tiles are not available, plain or scalloped-edge metal tags with a hole for attaching the chain work just as well and are even quicker to assemble. Search the Internet for companies selling them for industrial use—available in all sorts of fun colors and shapes—or try the scrapbooking section of your local craft and hobby store.

FLEA MARKET DISPLAY

ENCOURAGE BROWSING BY DISPLAYING YOUR PHOTOGRAPHS IN AN ENTIRELY NEW WAY. Here, dozens of unframed snapshots fill the racks of a rotating stand that once held the latest paperback books. Old fixtures like this one may take some ingenuity to find, so be open to all the possibilities. Look for stores that are going out of business or ask around at flea markets and secondhand shops.

GROWTH CHART

Use this playful chart to help you gauge how quickly your little saplings sprout. Not only will it report their height, it allows you to display a current picture of your kids at each growth milestone. This is a totally cut-and-paste craft project. Have fun choosing the background design. Let it match your child's room, incorporate favorite colors, or showcase a current passion. It's also a wonderful baby gift. You can find bookbinding linen at art supply stores in the bookmaking section. You could also make this project with a fine paper rather than fabric for a different look.

1   Make a color photocopy of the measuring tape on 11- x 17-inch paper in 3 sections, starting at 24 inches and ending at 65 inches.

2   Make the background design for the cardboard panels from your chosen decorative paper(s). Cut two 4-inch-wide strips per panel and glue them down with adhesive. Cut a 2-inch-wide strip of ruled paper and glue it down the center of each panel. If you are using decorative stickers that need to be under the measuring tape (as with our trains), apply them now.

3   To cover the panels of illustration board, lay 1 piece of the bookbinding linen facedown on the work surface; center 1 sheet of illustration board on it. Create mitered corners by removing any excess fabric at the corners with scissors (see diagram, next page). Fold over the top and bottom edges of the fabric and glue down with PVA glue. Repeat for left and right edges, making sure the fabric is smooth on the back side of the panel. Place waxed paper over the entire panel, cover with a weight, and let dry. Repeat for the remaining 2 panels.

4   **To hinge the panels together:** Stack the 3 cloth-covered boards, cloth sides faceup, edges aligned, and each panel separated by strips of ¼-inch-thick cardboard spacers. Cut 2 lengths of ribbon, each 48 inches long. Apply PVA glue down the length of the ribbon, leaving 6 inches bare at one end (use a scrap of cardboard to spread the glue evenly). Place the ribbon 2 inches from one edge, glue side against the linen, with the glueless 6 inches protruding at top; press in place. Wrap the bottom end of the ribbon around to the other side of the panel and press in place. Repeat with the second ribbon. Slide out the spacers. Remove any glue seepage with a damp sponge. Cover the ribbon with waxed paper, then a weight, and set aside to dry.

continued

IMAGES
Favorite snapshots, approx. 2½ x 3½ in.

PANTRY CHECKLIST
Metal ruler
Craft knife
Cutting mat
Scissors
Spray adhesive or an adhesive applicator
White craft glue (best-quality PVA glue)
Waxed paper
Sponge
Double-stick tape

MATERIALS
Measuring tape, to color copy (Step 1)
3 sheets of 9½- x 12½-in. lightweight
    cardboard or Bristol board
Sheets of gift wrap, wallpaper, or other
    decorative paper
1 large sheet of colorful ruled paper
Decorative stickers, optional
3 sheets of 10- x 13-in. illustration or
    binder's board
3 pieces of 16- x 19-in. bookbinding linen
    or tightly woven fabric
¼-in.-thick strips of cardboard, for
    spacers (Step 4)
3 yd. 1-in-wide satin ribbon
Clear self-stick photo corners
10-in.-long wooden or acrylic dowel,
    for hanging

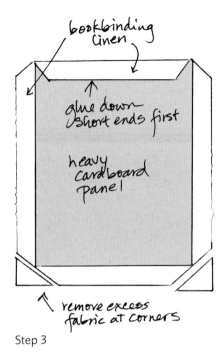

bookbinding
linen

glue down
short ends first

heavy
cardboard
panel

remove excess
fabric at corners

Step 3

5 To make hanging loops, fold over the top ends of the ribbon to form 2-inch loops; glue the ends down on the other side.

6 **To finish the panels:** Glue your 3 decorative paper panels to the fabric-covered panels, covering the ribbon ends and glued-down edges of the fabric. You will have about ¼ inch of linen showing on all edges. Cover each decorative panel with waxed paper, then a weight, and let dry overnight.

7 Trim away excess paper on the sections of photocopied measuring tape. Begin with the section for the bottommost panel of the chart; trim off any numbers below 24 inches. Hold that strip against the panel with the 24-inch mark at the very bottom and trim away any excess paper that extends beyond the top of the panel (on/around 36½ inches). Apply double-stick tape to the back of the strip and adhere it along the left side of the ruled paper with "24" at the very bottom. For the middle panel, place the center strip of measuring tape so it overlaps the 36-inch mark on the first panel; carefully mark the top and bottom edges and trim away excess paper. Adhere with tape as before. Repeat for the uppermost panel.

8 Slip the dowel through the loops at the top. It's ready to hang or present as a gift. (When you hang it, be sure that the bottom is 24 inches up from the floor.)

9 To add photos over time, place a clear photo corner on all four corners of your snapshot, position it where you like on the decorative borders of the chart, and press to apply, or glue in place for a more permanent bond.

PLAY For the background of each panel, select favorite decorative papers, color copies, or scans of patterned paper or fabric (we used 12- x 12-inch scrapbook sheets and added a decorative sticker border). The right and left halves can be solid or patterned, exactly the same or different. We used a different pattern for each half.

THROW PILLOW

DRESS UP YOUR SOFA, ARMCHAIR, OR BEDROOM WITH UNIQUE ACCENT PILLOWS, OR GIVE THEM AS GIFTS. Use one central image or arrange multiple, smaller pictures in a grid or collage. Lengths of ribbon add elegance and also prevent the edges of the image from fraying. For this pillow, Caroline chose a detail shot of Angkor Wat for its peaceful feeling and beautiful color. She found the perfect pillow case to match at a global import store, and spent a blissful hour at the art supply store choosing the cloth ribbon (for her, the hardest part of the whole project!). The image is printed onto fabric paper and, along with the trim, is adhered to the pillow with fabric glue—fast and easy.

ANTIQUE SHOES BABY QUILT

COMPUTER TOOLS
Digital camera
Image-editing software
Inkjet printer

PANTRY CHECKLIST
Tape
Sharp shears
Rotary cutter
Cutting mat
Quilting ruler
Household iron
Towel
Sewing machine with standard presser
     foot and even-feed (quilting) foot
Straight pins
Yardstick
Pencil

MATERIALS
9 objects to photograph, 1 for each
     square of the quilt
Fabric or paper (1 yd. per color) to use
     as the photo backgrounds
8½- x 11-in. paper-backed fine cotton
     sheets
White cotton/polyester thread
Fine sandpaper, for fabric templates
Crib size (45 x 60 in.) polyester batting

As a twist on an album quilt imprinted with old family photographs, we decided that one displaying digital images of our collection of antique baby shoes is a perfect gift for a new arrival. Photos of stuffed toys or the baby's immediate family (pets, too!) are other obvious themes. Two possible techniques for the transfer of images to fabric are iron-on transfers (see quilt, page 36) and direct printing, a more common method and the one we used. We prefer it for this project because the result is soft like printed fabric, much more suitable for a baby than the waxy surface of an iron-on transfer. This project isn't difficult. It just takes time. The end result is heirloom quality and, we think, worth the effort. Be sure to wash and dry your fabrics before cutting them out.

MAKING THE IMAGE SQUARES

1   Set up each photograph on a tabletop in bright, indirect light. Match each object to a background (iron smooth if fabric) and make a simple sketch of the final combinations as a reminder for shooting.

2   For each object, tape the background taut to the tabletop, and arrange the object in the center of the background, leaving sufficient empty background all around so you can adjust the cropping later on. NOTE: The images will be 8 inches square after the quilt is pieced together, 8½ inches square before sewing.

3   Photograph each object in natural light from a three-quarters angle, taking several exposures to be sure you have options. Use a high-resolution setting (our images were 7 x 10 inches at 300 dpi). Work reasonably quickly so the light doesn't change drastically.

4   Download the photos onto your computer. Select the 9 you like best and make a small color print (thumbnail) of each. Lay them out in the planned sequence for the quilt to be sure you like how they look together. It may be necessary to crop in or zoom back on some objects so they fill the square or match the scale of the rest. Number them in order 1–9 (see Diagram A, facing page). If needed, adjust the color of your image files (using the color controls in your image-editing software) so they all match.

5   With your printer set on thick-paper feed, print each image on a cotton-fabric sheet according to the manufacturer's instructions. Remove the paper backings and iron each

briefly on the wrong side to heat-set the image. Rinse the sheets, one at a time, in a pan of water 1 minute; lay them flat on a towel and let dry. Press each again.

QUILT FABRICS

Quilt top—washable, fine weave, pure cotton or 50/50 cotton polyester

For the backing: 1⅓ yd. 54-inch-wide white fabric

For the edging: 2 yd. accent fabric

For the outer border of the squares: 1 yd. white fabric

For accents A, B, C, D: ¼ yd. fabric each

Project Dimensions: Our finished quilt measures 44 inches square.

ASSEMBLING THE QUILT TOP

NOTE: All seams are ¼ inch and should be backstitched at both ends. Directions assume fabrics are pinned right sides together. Always press seams after you sew them (and press them toward the colored or image fabric, not the white fabric, so they don't show through). Do these steps every time and your quilt will finish square.

6 Make these templates from fine sandpaper: 7½-inch-square (for Fabric A), 2-inch square (for Fabrics B, C, D), 2 x 8 inch (for white fabric). Use them as follows: On your cutting mat, place a template rough-side down on the fabric and draw around it with pencil or fine chalk to mark the stitching line. Then place the quilting ruler over the sandpaper so it extends ¼ inch beyond the edge of the paper (to create a seam allowance). Cut the fabric with the rotary cutter using the edge of the ruler as a guide. You can cut as many as 4 layers of fabric at once using this method.

7 Cut out the following quantities and colors of fabric:

Fabric A: four 8-inch squares

Fabrics B and D: four 2½-inch squares of each

Fabric C: eight 2½-inch squares

White fabric: four strips 8 inches wide x 36 inches long, plus 24 strips that are each 2½ inches x 8½ inches

Edging fabric: Create bias strips by drawing cutting lines at a 45-degree angle that are spaced 3 inches apart (per Diagram B, below); seam strips together on the diagonal with a ½-inch seam allowance (you need 16 feet of bias edging).

continued

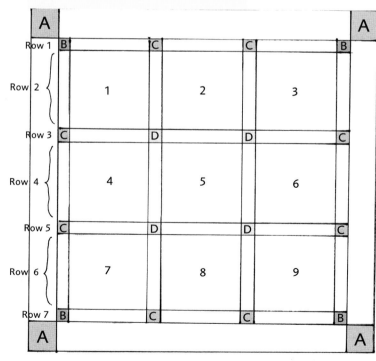

Diagram A

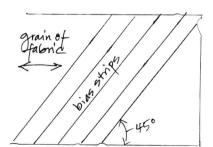

Diagram B

▶ **TIP** Don't be overwhelmed by all these steps; they're mostly sewing. Think of quilt squares and strips as building blocks. While you begin with many pieces, step-by-step you are joining them to form larger pieces that become very easy to stitch together. If you don't have a sewing machine, you can do sewing and quilting by hand. Instead of quilting to secure the layers, you can make tufts (decorative yarn knots; see page 36) at the corners of each square. ————

8 Trim your printed photographs to 8½ inches square, centering the object in the square. Pin an 8½- x 2½-inch strip of white fabric to the left edge of each image square. Also pin a strip to the right edges of Squares 3, 6, and 9. Using your sewing machine and standard presser foot, sew on these strips. You have now created Rows 2, 4, and 6. Press seams toward images.

9 Make the narrow bands for the alternating rows that will run between the image squares this way. Gather 2 squares of Fabric B, 4 squares of Fabric D, 6 squares of Fabric C, and the remaining 12 white strips; sew 1 small colored square to 1 end of each white strip. Following Diagram A, page 117, sew these strips together. For Rows 1 and 7, the sequence is (Fabric) B + white, C + white, C + white, plus a single square of accent color B. For Rows 3 and 5, assemble C + white, D + white, D + white, and a single square of color C.

10 To assemble the rows of the quilt, start by attaching Row 1 to the top of Row 2, and working down the quilt to Row 7. Carefully align the squares at the corners and pin or tack in place before sewing the full seam.

11 For the wider outer border, sew each square of Fabric A to the narrow end of one 8- x 36-inch white strip. Next, attach 1 assembled strip to each edge of the pieced top created in Step 10, shortening the white strip as needed to match up with the next corner square. Press all seams and surfaces well before quilting.

ASSEMBLING THE LAYERS

12 Iron the backing fabric. Lay it right side down on a large work surface. Unroll the batting on top of it, making sure that it is centered on the backing. Lay the pieced quilt top, right side up, on the batting, centering it side-to-side and 2 inches down from the top edge of the batting. Both batting and backing will be longer than the quilt top, which allows for any shifting of layers during quilting. Chop off the excess batting about 4 inches below the bottom of the quilt top. Carefully smooth out all layers with your hands and pin layers together every 6 inches.

13 **To quilt:** With your sewing machine and quilting foot, add rows of stitching "in the ditch" (where the squares are seamed together), using a basting stitch and always backstitching the ends of every seam. Start by quilting the seam that runs along the top of Row 1. Continue

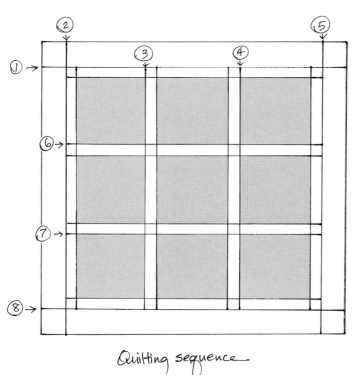

Quilting sequence

quilting, following the sequence shown in the diagram at left. After each row, check on the back side that the backing hasn't been caught or tucked. If it has, remove stitches, ease out fullness, and stitch that part again.

14 Smooth out the quilt on a large work surface. Carefully measure out from image squares and mark a line for the outer border at 7½ inches all around (this will include a 2-inch strip, plus 5 inches of the outer border, plus ½ inch for the edging). Pin all layers together and then stitch along this line with a basting stitch around all 4 edges of the quilt. Carefully cut your quilt to size by trimming through all layers ½ inch beyond the stitched line.

15 Add the bias edging starting at a corner on the back side of the quilt. Align the raw edge of the bias fabric with the edge of the quilt, right sides together, and pin in place. Stitch ½ inch from the edge (over top of previous stitching) through all layers. Turn the edging so it wraps around to the front side of the quilt. Turn under ½ inch of its free edge and pin the edging in place on the front of the quilt. Fold and tuck excess fabric at the corners under the edging, then topstitch (sew directly on the edging) all around to secure the edging. Hand-sew the final corner closed. Admire!

SYLVIA'S TOTE

Outrageous (or glamorous or quirky) photographs, pinked edges, and bold stitching turn a boring vinyl tote into a fun accessory any girl would lust after. Use one big shot or create an image collage that evokes an emotion or makes a personal fashion statement. Sewing a straight seam by machine or by hand is the only needle skill you need. All seam allowances are on the outside, a decorative detail that also makes assembly easier. Be sure to backstitch all seams ½ inch at both ends so they won't unravel later on.

A FEW POINTERS: Use 18-gauge vinyl if the tote is machine sewn, a slightly lighter weight if hand sewn. Vinyl is sticky and can "grab" the presser foot of your sewing machine, causing seams to bunch. Eliminate the problem by using a special foot that glides over the vinyl or by stitching over sewing tissue. Both are available at sewing centers.

1 With your image-editing software, crop and size your images so they will be 10¼ in. wide x 11 in. high at 200 dpi minimum. Print them at home or burn a CD of the files and have them printed at a service bureau. Or reproduce your images to size on a color photocopier.

2 For the front and back image panels, cut 4 vinyl pieces, each 12 x 13 inches. For the side gussets, cut 2 vinyl strips, each 3½ x 13 inches. For the bottom, cut 1 vinyl strip, 3½ x 12 inches. For the handles, cut 2 vinyl strips, each 3 x 15 inches.

3 Set your sewing machine's stitch length to Baste. Separate the Velcro strip; position 1 piece at the top center of 1 of the large vinyl panels, 1 inch below the edge. Stitch around the edges of the Velcro to attach it. Repeat with the other large panel, making sure the Velcro pieces line up. (These panels will form the inside of the tote.)

4 To construct the front and back (image) panels, sandwich 1 of your images between 2 of the large vinyl panels, one with Velcro, one plain (have the Velcro panel on the back side of the photo, Velcro facedown; see top diagram, next page). Line up all edges and sew across the top of both panels, just above the image. Sew 2 or more evenly space horizontal rows across the image. Then sew 2 evenly spaced vertical rows, sewing from top to bottom. Repeat with the remaining image and pair of large vinyl panels. With pinking shears, if desired, trim the top edge of each panel to create a decorative edge.

continued

IMAGES
Two digital images

COMPUTER TOOLS
Image-editing software
Inkjet or laser printer or photocopier

PANTRY CHECKLIST
Cutting mat
Rotary cutter or scissors
Metal ruler
Sewing machine fitted with a needle that sews leather and a presser foot with a nonstick coating or a roller foot
Pinking shears, optional

MATERIALS
¾ yd. medium or heavyweight vinyl
2-in.-long strip of 1-in.-wide hook-and-loop fastener (like Velcro) for the closure
Upholstery or nylon thread in a contrasting color

Project Dimensions: Our finished tote measures 12 in. wide x 13 in. high x 3½ in. deep.

Step 4

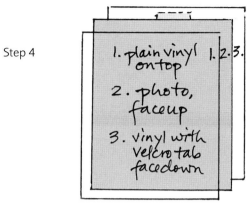

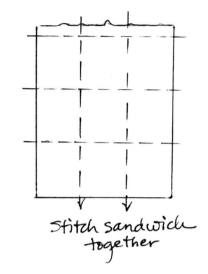

Step 7

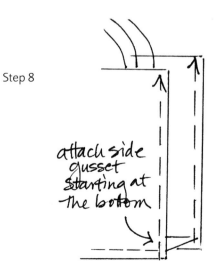

5 For the handles, fold one 3- x 15-inch vinyl strip in half lengthwise; stitch ⅛ inch from the cut edge along its entire length. Repeat for other handle.

6 On the inside of 1 image panel, position an end of one handle 1½ inches down from the panel's top edge and 2½ inches in from the side, with folded edge toward the center of the panel; secure it with 3 parallel rows of stitching, each about 1 inch long. Repeat to attach the other end of the handle. Secure the second handle to the other image panel in the same way.

7 For the bottom, lay the 3½- x 12-inch vinyl strip along the bottom edge of 1 of the image panels, image side down. Leaving a ½-inch seam, and beginning and ending ½ inch from each end of the strip, sew the pieces together with the seam allowance to the outside. Repeat to attach the bottom piece to the other image panel.

Step 8

8 **To finish:** Stitch each gusset strip to the tote bottom only, beginning and ending ½ inch from the ends of each strip. Stitch the gusset strips to the front and back panels, bottom to top. Pink the top edge of the gussets so they line up with the rest of the tote.

REARRANGED PHOTOGRAPH

HERE'S THE PERFECT USE FOR ALL THOSE "REJECT" PHOTOS THAT ARE CLUTTERING UP YOUR FILES. Divide a photo of any size into strips of any width, all equal or not. The artist made 2 copies of this 8- x 10-inch photo of a 1950s lamp (left). She spray mounted one of the copies to mat board and cut the other into 1-inch strips. Then she rearranged the cut-up strips 1 inch apart on the mounted image so the latter is alternately hidden and visible beneath the strips. A fun alternative is to assemble a group portrait from a stack of snapshots. Cut strips of the best parts of semigood shots (like where your mom looks great, but your brother is squinting, or of individual shots of friends who are never in the same place at the same time) and collage them into one image. Make your finished piece larger, if you like, by scanning it at high resolution, then having a copy shop or photo lab enlarge and print it.

THE EMPEROR'S BOX

AN OLD BOX MAKES A UNIQUELY BEAUTIFUL SHOWCASE FOR OBJECTS AND PHOTOGRAPHS. Meant to hang on the wall or stand upright, a shadow box is an ideal place to tell a tale, commemorate a trip, or honor a person or relationship. On the facing page, the artist displays artifacts and images from her trip to the Forbidden City in Beijing, China. Elements from the life of the last emperor, Pu Yi, are glued into a vintage artist's paint box—period spectacles; Chinese calligraphic paper and brushes; powdered paint; fire jars; a glass slide of a water lily from the imperial garden; pictures of the emperor from 1917 and 1935; as well as her own photographs, snapped at the doorway to the Forbidden City. Simpler variations, like the box above, make perfect vacation souvenirs or gifts.

ACCORDION-FOLD BOOK

Book lovers as well as photographers will find this technique especially satisfying to learn. Not only do you create a beautiful showcase for your images, you also get an excellent introduction to the respected art of making true bound books. Crafting the fabric-wrapped covers, attaching the pleated pages, and finishing them with endpapers are traditional bookbinding techniques. Don't rush through this project. A beautiful portfolio is the reward for a few days of dedicated work.

① For the images: Decide on a sequence for the images. Our layout alternates full-panel (full-bleed) images with smaller ones surrounded by a soft color tint. Using your image-editing software, size and crop the image for the front cover so it will print 2 inches square. Print it on matte photo paper, trim, and set aside.

IMAGES
8 digital images at 300 dpi, for the interior
1 digital image at 300 dpi, for the front
    cover

COMPUTER TOOLS
Image-editing software
Inkjet or laser printer or photocopier

PANTRY CHECKLIST
Craft knife
Cutting mat
Metal ruler
Transparent tape
Pencil
Spray adhesive or an adhesive applicator
White craft glue
Waxed paper

MATERIALS
Matte photo paper
1 sheet heavyweight matte paper, at
    least 11 x 17 in.
Bone folder
2 panels of binder's board, each $4\frac{1}{4}$ x
    $5\frac{1}{2}$ in.
$\frac{1}{4}$ yd. medium-weight, tightly woven
    fabric (cotton or linen, preferably)
1 yd. $\frac{1}{4}$- or $\frac{1}{2}$-in.-wide grosgrain or satin
    ribbon, cut in 4 equal pieces for tie
    closures
2 sheets of medium or heavyweight
    handmade paper, each $4\frac{1}{4}$ x $5\frac{1}{2}$ in.,
    for endpapers

Project Dimensions: $4\frac{1}{4}$ x $5\frac{1}{2}$ in. when closed; opens to $40\frac{1}{2}$ in. long.

► **TIP** If your color printer holds 11- x 17-inch paper, you can save steps. Create the layout in 2 halves using your software, grouping the full-size images together and the bordered images together. Then print each group directly onto the final paper, cut them apart, and attach to the panels as directed. ─────────────

② Size and crop Images 1, 3, 5, and 7 so they print 4 x 5¼ inches high; print on matte photo paper. For Panels 2, 4, 6, and 8, create a new document that is 4 x 5¼ inches high. Open Image 2 and with the EYE DROPPER tool, choose an accent color from the photograph and switch to the new document. Choose COMMAND-A (MAC) OR CTRL A (PC) to select all. Use the FILL tool to fill the selected area with your chosen color; adjust the opacity of the color as you like (we chose a 20% tint). Return to the image file, copy Image 2 and paste it in the center of the new document. Save the file as Panel 2. Repeat to create Panels 4, 6, and 8. Print these on matte photo paper.

③ Trim all printouts to size using the guides on your cutting mat so the corners of the images are square.

④ From the large sheet of heavyweight matte paper, cut out two 5¼- x 17-inch rectangles. Butt them together at their narrow ends and join them on the back side with transparent tape to form a hinge. Starting at the hinge, mark a light pencil tick on the back side along the

continued

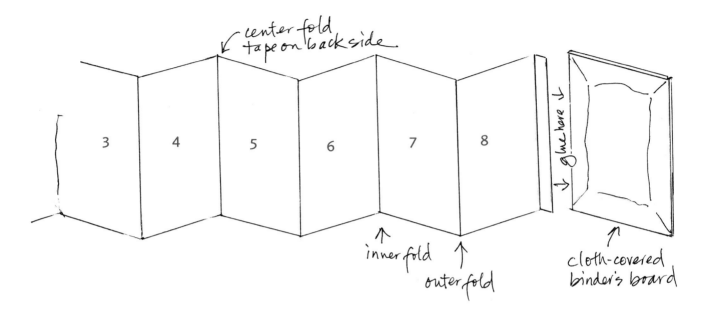

top and bottom long edges every 4 inches (measure very accurately). Connect corresponding top and bottom marks with a light pencil line to define the pages of the book. You should have eight 4- x 5¼-inch panels with 1 inch left over on either end. Score each pencil line by aligning the ruler along the line and running the bone folder along the ruler.

⑤ Using adhesive, affix each image to its corresponding panel. Start with a full-panel image and end with a bordered image. Leave the 1-inch strip at either end blank.

⑥ Use the following technique to fold the pages, making sure that all the bottom edges stay aligned as you create each fold. (Practice on a piece of scrap paper before you score and fold the actual accordion page.) Fold the panel at its halfway point (the tape hinge), with the images facing in. Make 1 fold on either side of the center fold; these will be outward folds, with the images facing out. The next 2 folds will be inward folds, and then the last 2 are outward folds.

⑦ **For the front cover:** On one 4¼- x 5½-inch binder's board panel, mark a 1½-inch-square window about 1¼ inches below the top edge and centered on the panel. Cut out the window with a craft knife.

⑧ Cut 2 pieces of fabric, each 5 x 6½ inches high. Using adhesive, affix 1 of the fabric pieces to the binder's board with the cutout. Place the board fabric-side down on the cutting mat, and cut an X in the fabric that covers the window, cutting from corner to corner

(see Slide-Mount Pins, page 55). Fold the fabric triangles to the back side of the board and glue them down. Fold the excess fabric around the edges of the board and glue it down. Center your cover photo in the window and tape or glue in place.

⑨ **For the back cover:** Glue the remaining piece of fabric to the remaining board, folding the excess fabric over the edges and gluing it to the back side.

⑩ Place front and back covers facedown on the work surface. Cover the back of each with waxed paper and then a weight, and set aside to dry for 30 minutes.

ASSEMBLING THE BOOK

⑪ On the unfinished sides of both front and back covers, center 1 length of ribbon on each vertical edge extending 1 inch onto the cover. Glue in place, weight, and dry as in Step 10.

⑫ To attach the accordion pages to the cover, apply glue to the blank 1-inch strip at each end of the image sequence; glue the beginning of the book to the inside of the front cover and the end of the book to the inside of the back cover (see diagram, opposite). If your images are faceup, the front cover (with window) will be at left. Weight and dry as in Step 10.

⑬ Glue a handmade paper sheet on the insides of both covers to finish them with end-papers. (Try to find a decorative paper that complements the visual theme. We used paper pressed with actual leaves to reflect the landscape photos.) Weight and let dry thoroughly.

PLAY As the book has pages of sorts, and a sequence, it lends itself well to time-lapse imagery or anything similar—the puppy growing up, a friend's surprise shower, or panoramic shots of a favorite view. Change the look by using handmade paper instead of fabric for the covers and/or a button closure instead of ribbon.

KITCHEN CLOCK

IMAGES
12½-in.-sq. digital image at 300 dpi

COMPUTER TOOLS
Image-editing software

PANTRY CHECKLIST
2-in.-wide brushes
Fine sandpaper
Scissors
Pencil
Masking tape
Measuring tape
Small watercolor brush
Needle-nose pliers, for clock assembly

MATERIALS
Bulldog Ultra Coating spray
12-in.-sq. wooden clock face,
    1 quartz clock movement,
    1 set 4½-in. hands
1 qt. latex primer
Acrylic paints, to finish exposed edges
    and for touch-ups
Acrylic matte medium
Cardboard
Paper, for template
D-ring and screws
Numbers: white, metal, or painted
    thumbtacks, or self-adhesive
    numbers (1–12)
Picture hanger

It's always cherry blossom time or your baby's bedtime or the good old summertime on this strikingly graphic clock. Pick a favorite time of year or day and have fun with it. A photo with an obvious center point, such as this extreme close-up of a lime tree blossom that Laura used to reflect her love of gardening, is a good choice, but not a must. Simple, bold images are most readable, but you can use a busy one if your number markers really stand out.

1 With your image-editing software, size and crop your image so it can be printed at 100% of final size. Burn a CD of the file and have a service bureau print the image with an inkjet printer on white canvas. Spray the printed canvas completely with Bulldog Ultra Coating. Let dry 24 hours.

2 Prime the front and back of the wooden clock with latex primer; let dry. Sand the surfaces smooth and wipe off any dust. Apply a contrasting color acrylic paint to the outer edges of the clock that won't be covered by the image. Paint the clock hands with acrylic paint, if desired; let dry.

3 Trim the printed canvas to exactly 12½ inches square. Coat the flat surface only of the wooden base with acrylic matte medium. Lay the canvas carefully on it so the center of the image is at the center of the clock (it may help to first punch a tiny hole in the exact center of the canvas, match it to the hole in the clock face, and align both by pushing a pencil through both holes). Lay cardboard over the clock face and weight it; let dry 30 minutes.

4 To glue the sides, cut a triangle from each loose corner of the canvas so you can glue down the corners without any overlap. Cover 1 sloping side of the clock face at a time with acrylic medium. Press the canvas firmly in place until it adheres; repeat for the other 3 sides. If necessary, with acrylic paints and a small brush, touch up the image and also paint the corners where the canvas meets.

5 Mask off the painted wooden border of the clock with tape. To seal the edges of the canvas, apply 2 coats of acrylic medium to the sloped edges of the clock face (we tinted the medium with a dab of black acrylic paint per spoonful of medium to mask the transition from clock face to border). Apply 1 coat of untinted acrylic medium to the face of the clock to protect the printed canvas. Let all dry.

continued

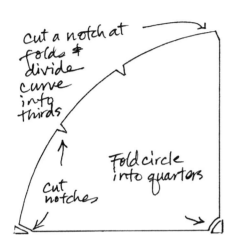

cut a notch at
folds &
divide
curve
into
thirds

↑
cut
notches

Fold circle
into quarters

► **TIP** To space numbers evenly on the clock face, make a round paper template of the correct diameter. Fold the circle in half, then in half again. Divide the outer circumference into thirds per the diagram above. Cut a notch at each mark and at the fold points. Snip off a bit of the tip. Unfold the circle, center it on the clock face, and secure it with a pencil as you do in Step 3. Align one of the folds exactly vertical, then carefully mark on the clock face at each notch. ─────────────

(6) Attach the D-ring to the center top edge of the back of the clock.

(7) Put a pencil mark on the 12 spots for the numbers. Push in a thumbtack or affix a number at each mark.

(8) Install the clockworks according to the manufacturer's instructions, protecting the face with cardboard while you do, then attach the hands.

PLAY We used a service bureau to print the image on canvas from a digital file burned onto a CD, as it was too large for most home printers, which only accept 8½- x 11-inch canvas sheets. If you use a smaller clock or divide the clock face into quarters, each with its own image (such as 4 different faces, places, or seasons), you can print it yourself. Or, if your printer can produce 11- x 17-inch color images, use heavy paper stock or canvas-textured paper instead.

REPURPOSED WINDOW FRAME

AN OLD WINDOW RESCUED FROM A HOME RENOVATION PROJECT OR A SAL-VAGE YARD REINVENTS AS A MULTIPICTURE FRAME. Have new panes of window glass installed professionally (use all glass or a combination of glass and mirror as we did). Then, select images from a series or ones that complement each other, measure the panes carefully, and print your images to size onto heavy photo paper. Because our prints are large (15 inches square), we had them printed at a photo lab onto glossy photo paper. We held the images in place on the panes temporarily with double-sided tape, then sealed all edges with ¼-inch white masking tape.

▶ 4

TILE-TOPPED PLANT STAND

TILE-TOPPED PLANT STAND

IMAGES
11-in.-sq. (final size) digital image at
      300 dpi

COMPUTER TOOLS
Image-editing software
Inkjet or laser printer (not a Hewlett
      Packard laser printer for this project)

PANTRY CHECKLIST
2-in.-wide disposable brushes
Newspaper
Rotary cutter
Metal ruler
Cutting mat
Paper towels
2- or 3-in. trim roller and foam cover
Pencil
5-Minute Epoxy Gel

MATERIALS
1 qt. clear satin fast-drying polyurethane
      finish
12-in.-sq. x 24-in.-high unfinished
      wooden plant stand
Fine sandpaper
Aqua-Slide Decal Paper
Krylon Clear Acrylic Spray
4 small (4- in.-sq.) tiles, for test prints
12-in.-sq. unglazed ceramic or stone tile
      (sold as 12 in. sq., but actual size is
      about 11¾ in. sq.)

This table was envisioned as a plant stand by our green thumb, Laura. But when it was finished, she couldn't bear to obscure the image—the crumbling, vine-tangled ruins of Pompeii—with a plant! It found new life outdoors next to a comfortable, fog-weathered deck chair. Garden, landscape, and still-life shots, in color or black-and-white, lend themselves beautifully to this technique. Laura chose a duotone look for her image (see "Antiquing" a New Photograph, page 63), but any style looks great. For good buys on ceramic, stone, and marble tiles, check architectural salvage yards.

1 Brush on 2 coats of polyurethane to the plant stand. Let it dry overnight between coats; before applying the second coat, sand the wood lightly to remove rough spots and any drips.

2 Make 4 test prints: Using your image-editing software, crop an 8- x 8-inch square from your image that includes a range of light to dark tones; use SAVE AS to save it as a new document (you do not want to permanently change the original file). Using the RECTANGULAR MARQUEE TOOL, select one quarter of the image at a time, making 3 color variations to your image, and leaving one quarter untouched. Some variations to try: Increase the contrast, adjust the coloring using the HUE slider (select HUE/SATURATION under ADJUST COLORS), reduce the saturation (with the SATURATION slider) to create a tinted black-and-white image. Save your file again.

3 Set your printer for glossy media (paper) and print your test images onto the glossy side of the decal paper; let dry several minutes. If your color looks too transparent (thin), you may need to try other media (paper) settings for your printer or adjust the saturation of your image with your image-editing software.

4 ⚠ In a well-ventilated area and wearing a mask, place your print, image side up, on a newspaper. Spray on a heavy coat of acrylic spray, thoroughly covering the whole sheet from edge to edge. The paper should look shiny and wet, but the coating should not be so thick that it puddles and runs. Let it dry completely. Repeat twice more, spraying in opposite directions each time. Let the final coat dry at least 8 hours or overnight.

5 Using the rotary cutter, ruler, and cutting mat, trim the images, leaving a narrow white margin all around for easier handling.

TIP While the tile you use makes all the difference, there is no right or wrong here, just varying effects. Also remember: the color of the tile will show through, especially in the white areas of your photo, which transfer clear. Darker stone produces more subtle contrasts. Smooth tiles are easier to handle, but you might prefer the rustic thickness of rough, porous stone as Laura did. Do tests on small tiles first and see what you like.

⑥   **For each test tile:** Make sure the tile is clean. Place the tile on paper towels so it won't slide around. Take 1 test image and set it in a bowl of warm (not hot) water for a few minutes until the backing paper starts to loosen (it's ready when a bubble forms between the decal film and paper backing). With the image still floating in the water, carefully peel back and tear off 1 corner of the backing paper.

⑦   Lift the decal paper from the water and align it on your tile, right side up (use the clear corner as a guide). Hold down the outside margin in the clear corner with your finger and slide the rest of the backing paper from under the film. Once the backing is removed, carefully realign the film on the tile. Using the foam roller, work out any trapped air bubbles and completely adhere the film to the tile; use light pressure and work from the center of the image out.

⑧   Repeat 3 more times for the remaining test tiles. Set all 4 tiles aside to dry for at least 24 hours. The white areas will be clear when completely dry. (If you finish them with polyurethane—see Step 13—and back them with cork, they'll make great coasters.)

⑨   **For the final full-size image:** Choose your favorite test image (we chose one that was desaturated some). Using your image-editing software, adjust the color and contrast of the full-size image to match the test image.

⑩   In order to seam the image, you will need to divide the final image vertically and print each half on a separate sheet of decal paper (see Festive Votives, Steps 1 and 2, page 59, for directions). Spray them well, per Step 4, and let dry thoroughly.

⑪   Once you have trimmed each half of the image so they perfectly align, trim the margins of both photos down to ¼ inch on all other sides. On the 12-inch tile, make a light pencil line where the 2 image halves will seam together.

⑫   Following Steps 6–8, soak and apply 1 image half to the tile at a time, aligning each half along the pencil line. For the other half, start by aligning the image seam first so you can carefully match up the halves before letting the rest of the film make full contact with the tile. Carefully roll out any air bubbles from the center out. Let dry at least 24 hours.

⑬   Adhere the tile to the tabletop with epoxy; let dry 15 minutes, then seal the top and sides of the tile with at least 2 coats of polyurethane.

PLAY We've given you directions for a plant stand of the exact dimensions of ours, but you can easily apply this technique to a low table, a bench, or coffee table of any size, using a single tile or multiples. If the base is a flea-market find, sand it well to smooth the surface or the glue won't adhere.

VELLUM LAMPSHADES

IMAGES
Digital image(s) at 300 dpi

COMPUTER TOOLS
Scanner or digital camera
Image-editing software
Inkjet or laser printer or photocopier

PANTRY CHECKLIST
Pencil
Craft knife
Cutting mat
Metal ruler
Scissors

MATERIALS
An old, out-of-print book
3 or 4 stems of your favorite flowers
1 large sheet of handmade paper, as
    background for the flower image
Translucent iron-on transfer paper
8½- x 11-in. vellum paper
Plain 4-sided white lampshade
Card stock or thin cardboard, larger
    than 1 panel of the shade, for the
    cropping template
Decorative paper (tissue weight),
    for the joining strips
Vellum tape

Project Dimensions: Each panel of our
lampshade is 3½ x 8 x 7 in. high.

Shine a light on your creative talents by covering a ready-made lampshade with a beautiful image printed on vellum paper. Caroline crafted ours by using iron-on transfer paper to overlay Laurie's photograph of calla lilies onto a page from an old French book she found at the flea market. We love the look of furled flowers in soft shades against the graceful old type (so much so that we took it to our nearest copy shop, enlarged it, and framed it as a print). The new image was scanned and then, using image-editing software, played with to produce a different version for each panel of the shade. You can skip the layering steps if you already have a suitable image (or images, if you want to use different ones for each panel), but it's a neat trick to have in your repertoire.

NOTE: If you already have an image you'd like to use as is, scan it, if necessary, per Step 4, then begin with Step 5. To create a layered image like Laurie's:

① Select a page you love from an old book and set it aside. If you're reluctant to rip out the page, you will need a scanner to complete Step 4.

② Place a few of your favorite flowers on the sheet of handmade paper and photograph them. If you don't shoot digitally, get a print made and scan it at 300 dpi. Using your image-editing software, size the image so it's a bit smaller than the page you've chosen. Print it out onto transfer paper.

continued

▶ **TIP** You can do this entire project at home or at a copy shop with a color photocopier. You'll need a print, rather than a digital image. You can reduce and color copy the image directly onto transfer paper. After you make the transfer, play around with different sizes and sections in black-and-white until you have four 8½- x 11-inch variations that you like. Then make color copies of them on vellum paper and take it from there. ────

③ Position the transfer image facedown onto your book page and iron it on, following the manufacturer's instructions. Be careful not to scorch the paper.

④ Scan your newly adorned book page and save as a JPEG file that is 8½ x 11 inches at 300 dpi.

⑤ To end up with 4 different looks for the sides of the shade, crop the image and save it as a new file. Open the original file again, crop the image another way, and save it as a new file. Repeat twice more, until you have created 4 different versions of the same image. Try to keep the resolution at least 150 dpi, more if you want to retain maximum sharpness (we prefer the soft look, which is pretty much inevitable with vellum anyway).

⑥ Print the 4 variations you like best onto vellum paper and set aside. (You may need to experiment with the media settings in your PRINT dialog box to get the best result.)

⑦ To make the cropping template, hold the card stock against 1 panel of the shade. With a pencil, trace the perimeter of the panel. Using your craft knife, cutting mat, and straight-edge ruler, cut out the cardboard panel you've just outlined, leaving a cropping window the same size as one panel of the shade.

⑧ Select an area of each vellum image that you think would look most interesting on the shade this way: Lay the template on the image and move it around until you find an area (and an angle) that you like. Trace the shape and cut it out. Repeat for all 4 sides.

ASSEMBLING THE LAMPSHADE

⑨ Measure 1 panel of your lampshade and cut the following strips from the decorative tissue paper: four strips ¾-in.-wide by the width of the bottom edge, four strips ¾-in.-wide by the width of the top edge, and four strips ¼-inch-wide by the height of your shade.

⑩ **Secure your vellum panels to the lampshade as follows** (see diagram, left): Line up the bottom of 1 vellum panel with the bottom of 1 side of the lampshade. Fold a bottom strip in half lengthwise (if your paper has a "right" side, it should be out). Press a strip of vellum tape firmly along the inside of each half and then pull it up (the glue will be transferred to the paper). Center the crease of the folded strip against the bottom edge of the lampshade. Press the top half of the strip against the vellum panel first (so you can be sure the visible side is straight), then wrap the other side of the strip around the bottom of the shade and onto its inner side. Smooth out any bubbles.

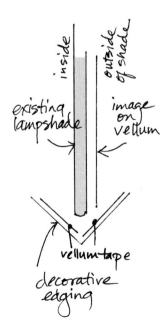

inside · outside of shade

existing lampshade · image on vellum

vellum tape

decorative edging

Repeat this process for the top of the panel, using a strip the width of the top edge. You will now have 1 vellum panel attached to 1 side of the lampshade. Repeat for the remaining 3 panels, being sure to line up your decorative strips so they form a continuous line around the top and bottom of the shade.

(11) To secure the vertical seams where the panels meet, apply vellum tape to the underside of each of the remaining strips. Place the center of the strip along the vertical seam where the 2 panels meet. Press each side down. Repeat for the remaining 3 seams.

PLAY   Experiment with the cropping boundaries to create larger or smaller versions of a section so the scale of your final images varies, as it does here. You can also print your image at the original size, provided it's large enough to cover one side of the shade. Or, you can choose 4 different images that work as a group, 1 for each side.

CARLA'S HANGING MURAL

USING YOUR HOME PRINTER YOU CAN CREATE A LARGE-SCALE PHOTOGRAPHIC WORK THAT WOULD BE A FOCAL POINT IN ANY ROOM. This 50- x 60-inch wall mural (displayed in reverse, below) is comprised of colorful photographs from the artist's trip to Morocco as well as pictures of her own oil paintings. She printed 24 images onto 8- x 10-inch sheets of premium photo paper (use heavyweight paper for best image quality and to reduce curling), then strung them together top and bottom through tiny pinholes using self-fastening loops of plastic thread from the hardware store, creating 6 strips of 4 panels each. For display, insert a wooden dowel through the loops and hang it with wire from a picture rail. Make your mural larger or smaller by changing the paper size or number of panels. To devise a dramatic room divider, draw, paint, stamp, print, or color the reverse side of each panel.

FOLDING SCREEN

FOLDING SCREEN

IMAGES
5 different images at 300 dpi, or from 1 to 36 images

COMPUTER TOOLS
Image-editing software
Scanner or photocopier
Inkjet printer

PANTRY CHECKLIST
36-in. metal ruler
Felt-tip marker (flat tip)
Transparent tape
Craft knife (with spare blades)
Large cutting mat
Pencil
Freezer paper
Clean sponges
4 in. foam roller and replaceable foam covers

MATERIALS
3-fold wooden screen with rice-paper-like fabric panes
Legion Photo Matte Paper
Scrap paper, for planning the design
1 large or 2 small sheets $3/16$-in. foam-board
Canvas tarp or drop cloth
Crafter's Pick 1100 Bookbinding Glue
Paint tray for 4-in. roller
6 masonite or heavy flat cardboard panels, cut to fit exactly into the squares of the screen

Project Dimensions: Each panel of our screen is 18 in. x 6 ft. high overall.

This stunning screen may look like a daunting project for the weekend photocrafter, but its designer, Laura, promises that only you will know how easily it went together. Everyone else will be terrifically impressed. She used a purchased Japanese-style wooden screen backed with fabric that she covered with photos of desert plant forms. The originals, platinum prints with a lovely softness, were rescanned for this project and scaled much larger. She retained most of their borders because she liked the effect inside the black lattice frame of the screen.

1 **Create your design:** Using ruler and marker, draw a diagram of the screen on scrap paper, using a scale of 1 inch = 1 foot. Mark the screen frame and lattice on the diagram. Print or photocopy a small color version (thumbnail) of each image; rearrange and play around with these on your diagram until you get a layout that you like. (It's easier if a photo fills the entire square, but it's not necessary; stop partway if it looks good. Leave some squares image-free, a nice pause in the overall design that helps to separate images that might otherwise visually clash. Avoid overlapping images; if multiple layers of paper are glued in one square the paper could warp.)

2 Resize or recopy images until they fit the grid in a pleasing way, then tape or glue everything in place on the diagram. You will reproduce this design on your actual screen.

3 Scan images to size or resize digital images to fit your design. Print images onto matte photo paper (if the design is busy, keep track of your design by numbering the squares on the diagram and then lightly mark the back of each print in pencil with the corresponding number).

4 Lay the tarp out on a large table or hard-surface floor; carefully rest the screen on the tarp. Complete 1 panel of the screen at a time, as follows:

5 On the back of the screen (the side without the lattice strips), the cloth will be indented below the framing. To make the back level, measure the area of white cloth that shows (ours is 15 x 50 inches), and cut the foamboard into panels that fit snugly into this indentation, covering it from top to bottom; temporarily tape in place. This will make a level surface to push against when you are gluing from the top side. You will use the same foamboard backing for the entire screen, moving it from one panel to the next as you glue.

continued

► **TIP** If you plan to enlarge your images greater than 18 inches (the width of 1 panel of the screen), we highly recommend that you have high-resolution scans made at a service bureau for the best quality. For prints larger than 11 x 17 inches, find a service bureau that does inkjet printing on rolls of paper as we did. The same stock, however, comes in all sorts of paper sizes from 8½- x 11-inch sheets to 100-foot rolls so you can use whatever equipment you have. Just know you'll need a lot more prints if they are all small. ———————————

6 For the front of the screen, you will cut each photograph to fit its specific square, using your diagram as your guide. Start by cutting a straight vertical edge and a 90-degree corner to the photo. Carefully place it in its corresponding square on the screen (a must for each photo, as it is unlikely that the squares are true—ours sure weren't!). Mark with pencil where it touches the other 2 sides of the square. Place the photo on a cutting mat and cut against the metal ruler at the pencil marks, using a firm steady stroke. Set the trimmed photograph into its square and go on to the next. Change blades often so the knife is never dull. When you have an entire panel done, step back and confirm that it matches your sample design, and that nothing is misplaced or upside down.

7 **To glue the images in place:** Lay a large sheet of freezer paper (considerably larger than the size of an image) on a work surface. Pour a small puddle of glue in the paint tray. Dampen the foam roller with water and squeeze out any excess. Remove 1 image at a time from its square and place it facedown on the freezer paper.

8 Dip the roller in glue and roll a thin, even layer of glue onto the image back, covering all edges. Carefully lift up the image to make sure that no glue seeped onto the front (remove any that has with a damp sponge). Place it carefully back in its square on the screen and press all edges in place. Check again for glue seepage, wiping it away if necessary, as before. Place a piece of masonite, smooth side down, over the glued image and cover with a weight. Let set 15 to 20 minutes, then remove boards and weights. (If you stop work for more than 20 minutes, return the glue to the jar and wash all tools in warm water.)

9 Repeat with the rest of the images, using a clean area of freezer paper for each, removing boards and weights as each image sets.

PLAY The easiest approach is to use a different photo for each square, repeating any that you really love. Decide if the screen will be a bold accent or a background accessory and choose images accordingly. The smaller the imagery, the closer you must be to see it clearly, but from a distance it will yield a nice overall pattern. Consider color as a theme; incorporate various exposures and details of a particularly gorgeous sunrise, for example, or the warm tones of autumn leaves. Or treat the screen as one scene, such as a snowy street, a beach boardwalk, or a favorite corner of your garden.

COLLAGE UNDER GLASS

A COFFEE OR SIDE TABLE WITH A GLASS TOP IS THE PERFECT PLACE TO SHOW OFF YOUR CHERISHED PHOTOS. Remove the glass, and on the tabletop, arrange a group of images to create funny, elegant, abstract, or nostalgic tableaus. Or simply display the highlights from your most recent vacation. Caroline chose favorite vintage photographs in a variety of shapes and sizes from her family albums. Consider how people will approach the table—pictures facing in multiple directions look cool. When your layout is perfect, simply reinstall the glass top over the photos.

SHOWER CURTAIN

THIS DELIGHTFUL CURTAIN IS THE BEST REASON TO TAKE A SHOWER WE CAN THINK OF, and worth its somewhat hefty price. A service bureau that prints photographs on very lightweight vinyl does most of the work. Check the yellow pages for one that makes banners. They'll supply the vinyl, hem it, and install the grommets along the top. Use any image you like, but water themes—like this one of Laurie's two sons playing in an old metal washtub—look best. Measure your existing shower curtain and scan your image at the resolution required by your service bureau for printing on vinyl. (We scanned this one, for a 72- x 72-inch curtain, to be 100 dpi at full size.) Make a CD of the file and drop it off at the bureau; your shower curtain should be ready in about a week.

RESOURCES

 Equipment

Adobe Systems
Manufacturer/online catalog
800-833-6687 (toll free)
www.adobe.com
Makers of Photoshop and Photoshop
Elements software. A good resource for
support and technical help.

Calumet Photographic
Retail stores/online and direct-mail catalogs
890 Supreme Drive
Bensenville, IL 60106
800-225-8638 (toll free)
www.calumetphoto.com
Photographic and digital equipment and
supplies, plus books and videos.

Epson America
Manufacturer/online catalog
PO Box 93012
Long Beach, CA 90806
800-463-7766
www.epson.com
Makers of a wide range of inkjet and laser
printers, photo printers, scanners, inks, and
papers. Web site offers extensive support,
advice, and project ideas.

Imaging Resource
Information
www.imaging-resource.com
Reviews and comparisons of digital cameras
and accessories plus photography tutorials.

PC Connection
Mac Connection
Online catalog
888-800-0323 (toll free)
www.pcconnection.com

800-986-4420 (toll free)
www.macconnection.com
Wide assortment of digital equipment: computers, scanners, monitors, cameras, software,
memory cards, and every possible accessory.

PCMall/MacMall
Retail stores/online and direct-mail catalogs
PCMall: 800-555-6255 (toll free)
www.pcmall.com
MacMall: 800-622-6255 (toll free)
www.macmall.com
A wide selection and good prices for digital
equipment of all kinds.

Steve's DigiCams
Digital Photography Review
Information
www.steves-digicams.com
www.dpreview.com
The best places to start when researching digital cameras. Extensive glossaries of terms,
reviews, and stats on every make and model,
buying guides, comparison pricing, reference
section with tips and techniques for improving
your digital photography skills.

 Images and Fonts

Dover Publications
Publisher/online and direct-mail catalogs
http://store.doverpublications.com
CD-ROM/book sets with permission-free art.
Most art and book stores stock Dover products.

iStockphoto
Online catalog
866-478-6251 (toll free)
www.istockphoto.com

A great resource for royalty-free imagery; over
a million photos available for a few dollars each.

Phil's Fonts
Online and direct-mail catalogs
800-424-2977 (toll free)
Fax: 301-260-2277
www.philsfonts.com
A very complete font shop with a huge range
of typeface styles and prices.

Photos.com
Online catalog
800-482-4567 (toll free)
www.photos.com
Professional royalty-free stock photos by
monthly subscription. A good deal if you need
many images.

Two Peas in a Bucket
Online catalog
888-896-7327 (toll free)
www.twopeasinabucket.kaboose.com
A scrapbooking site that's lots of fun to
browse, with very inexpensive fonts.

VintageClipArt.com
Online catalog
207-415-6459
www.vintageclipart.com
Royalty-free CD collections of full-color
vintage clip art and Victorian images.

The Vintage Workshop
Online catalog/distributor to retail stores
913-341-5559
www.thevintageworkshop.com
Inexpensive vintage images for computer
crafting. Downloadable files, CDs, and licensing
available. Check their Web site for retail
sources.

Archival Materials

Archival Methods
Manufacturer/online catalog
866-877-7050 (toll free)
www.archivalmethods.com
A great source for archival storage cases, display binders, and presentation materials.

Hollander's
Retail store/online catalog
410 North Fourth Avenue
Ann Arbor, MI 48104
734-741-7531
www.hollanders.com
Wonderful retail store and online catalog specializing in bookbinding materials, including book cloth, bone folders, archival glues and tapes; over 1200 decorative and handmade papers; watercolor paper; kits for making books and photo albums.

Light Impressions
Online and direct-mail catalogs
800-828-6216 (toll free)
www.lightimpressionsdirect.com
The world's leading resource for fine archival storage, display, and presentation materials for negatives, transparencies, CDs, photographs, artwork, and documents. Selection includes UV-filtering glass, archival mat board, frames, photo albums, linen tape, slide mounts, and glues.

Artist's and Craft Materials

A.C. Moore
Retail stores/limited online catalog
www.acmoore.com
120 stores stocked with arts and crafts materials including scrapbooking, artists' materials, framing, and kids' crafts. Their Web site offers numerous project ideas and instructions.

Create for Less
Online catalog
866-333-4463 (toll free)
www.createforless.com
Over 50,000 brand-name craft supplies, discount prices, and bulk quantities. Carries all sorts of alphabet stickers.

Daniel Smith
Retail stores/online and direct-mail catalogs
4150 First Avenue South
Seattle, WA 98134
800-426-6740 (toll free)
www.danielsmith.com
Extensive selection of artist's papers, craft supplies, adhesives, drawing materials, and more.

Dick Blick Art Materials
Retail stores/online and direct-mail catalogs
800-933-2542 (toll free)
www.dickblick.com
Wide selection of art and craft supplies; archival storage boxes, papers, and shipping cases; bookbinding cloth, board, glues; Bristol, foam, illustration, and art boards; kits for making books and photo albums; Lascaux varnishes and sealers, pre-coated blueprint paper, Marshall's Photo Oils (also available at Flax and Michaels).

Flax Art & Design
Retail store/online and direct-mail catalogs
1699 Market Street
San Francisco, CA 94103
888-352-9278 (toll free)
www.flaxart.com
Every art and craft supply you can think of; a particularly great selection of photo albums; decorative, handmade, and watercolor papers; gift and stationery items.

Michaels
Retail stores/online catalog
800-642-4235 (toll free)
www.michaels.com
Very extensive selection. Web site offers how-to information and shows completed projects.

Office Depot
Retail stores/online and direct-mail catalogs
800-463-3768 (toll free)
www.officedepot.com
Good buys on inkjet and standard papers, printer inks, and some specialty papers (like self-adhesive transparency film).

Pearl Paint
Retail stores/online and direct-mail catalogs
308 Canal Street
New York, NY 10013
800-221-6845 (toll free)
www.pearlpaint.com
The unbeatable selection of art and craft supplies includes extensive paint and paper choices. The stores carry much more than the online catalog. Terrific direct-mail catalog.

Rag Shop
Retail stores
973-423-1303
www.ragshop.com
A wide selection of value-priced merchandise for crafters: fabrics to floral to framing.

Sunshine Discount Crafts
Online and direct-mail catalogs
800-729-2878 (toll free)
www.sunshinecrafts.com
Wide range of craft supplies including lampshades and night-light kits, glues, multipurpose sealers, and scrapbook supplies.

Wilde-Ideas Paper Arts Supplies
Retail store/online catalog
625 Grand Central Street
Clearwater, FL 33756
866-818-9345 (toll free)
www.wilde-ideas.com
Xyron machines, adhesives and tapes, books, papers, paints, tools.

► Specialized Craft Materials

The Crafty PC
Online catalog
732-873-8055
www.thecraftypc.com
Unusual materials for photo prints: balloons, blank playing cards, blank clocks, pennants, inkjet fabric sheets, calendar kits, greeting cards and envelopes, baby bibs.

Creative Imaginations
Distributor
800-942-6487 (toll free)
www.cigift.com
Scrapbooking supplies galore, including Pastel Negative Strips.

Hemmi Papilio
Online catalog
817-489-5249
www.papilio.com
Terrific resource for inkjet and laser specialty films and papers, adhesive-backed paper and film, transfer paper, water slide decal paper, "waterproof" inkjet vinyl, printable metallics, magnetic paper, and numerous sealants.

Hollander's
Retail store/online catalog
410 North Fourth Avenue
Ann Arbor, MI 48104
734-741-7531
www.hollanders.com
Wonderful retail store and online catalog, specializing in bookbinding materials, including book cloth, bone folders, archival glues and tapes; over 1200 decorative and handmade papers; kits for making books.

Impress Rubber Stamps
Retail stores/online catalog
120 Andover Park East
Tukwila, WA 98188
206-901-9101
www.impressrubberstamps.com
Eyelets and eyelet setters, card and envelope sets, ribbons, small containers, photo bracelets and photo pendants, metal edge tags, and more.

InkAID
Online catalog
888-424-8167 (toll free)
www.inkaid.com
A coating (compatible with dye and pigment inks) that can be brushed or sprayed onto materials that aren't precoated for inkjet printing, including unsized paper, foil, and metal.

Jewelry Supply
Online catalog
916-780-9610
www.jewelrysupply.com
Jewelry-making materials of all kinds, including findings (bails, clasps, chains), charms, beads, cord and wire, needle-nose pliers, and more.

Lazertran
Online catalog
800-245-7547 (toll free)
www.lazertran.com
Use Lazertran Waterslide Decal Paper with printers and copiers to transfer imagery onto almost anything, including nonabsorbent reflective surfaces (glass, ceramic tiles, and shiny sheet metal) and silk fabric.

Making Memories
Distributor
801-294-0430
www.makingmemories.com
A great source for embellishments such as eyelets, paper tags and labels, brads, mesh and wire, alphabet stickers, envelopes and paper, mini books, and tags.

McMaster-Carr Supply Company
Retail stores/online catalog
330-342-3330
www.mcmaster.com
World's greatest online hardware store—over 450,000 items. Check their Web site for retail sources.

Photographers' Formulary
Retail store/online and direct-mail catalogs
PO Box 950, 7079 Highway 83 N.
Condon, MT 59826

406-754-2894
www.photoformulary.com
Photo chemistry, including cyanotype kits for amateur and professional photographers; also workshops, newsletter, technical help.

Prym
Manufacturer/distributor
www.dritz.com
Sewing, quilting, and craft supplies, including Dritz Color Snaps and cutting mats. Check their Web site for retail sources.

Scrapbook Creations
Online catalog
www.scrapbook-creations.com
Embellishments, cutting tools, and lots of papers and stickers, including a huge line of Sticko sticker products.

Transfer Technology
Online catalog
888-872-6706 (toll free)
www.transfertechnology.com
Transfer paper for inkjet printers and color copiers; blank products such as mouse pads, calendars, clocks, and place mats for imprinting.

Stampington & Company
Online catalog
www.stampington.com
877-782-6737 (toll free)
Good source for hard-to-find items like little glassine envelopes, metal tags, tiny tins, lamp kits, vellum paper, mesh bags, and wooden boxes, plus Narratives Negative Strips.

Walnut Hollow
Online catalog
800-950-5101 (toll free)
www.walnuthollow.com
High-quality unfinished wood products, including clock faces, hands, movements, and numbers, plus wooden boxes, trays, frames, signs, and more.

Adhesives, Sealers, & Laminates

3M
Manufacturer
888-364-3577 (toll free)
www.3m.com
Products for home and office, including tapes, glues, mounting materials, and laminating supplies. Maker of Scotch tape and 3M Super 77 Spray Adhesive.

Crafter's Pick
Online catalog
510-526-7616
www.crafterspick.com
Excellent craft glues, including Crafter's Pick The Ultimate, Crafter's Pick 1100 Bookbinding Adhesive (our favorite), and Memory Mount. Check their Web site for retail sources.

Daige
Online catalog
800-645-3323 (toll free)
www.daige.com
Adhesive and laminating systems for mounting photos, including Rollataq hand applicators.

Houston Art
Online catalog
800-272-3804 (toll free)
www.houstonart.com
Omni-Gel transfer medium and Mona Lisa Clear Cote sealer, other thinners and mediums.

Lamination Plus
Online catalog
888-225-9880 (toll free)
www.laminationplus.com
Leading source for laminators and laminating supplies.

Plaid
Manufacturer/distributor
800-842-4197 (toll free)
www.plaidonline.com
Creates and distributes over 5,000 craft materials and products, including Mod Podge glue/sealer, Royal Coat decoupage medium, and Picture This transfer medium.

This to That
Information
www.thistothat.com
Find the correct product to glue any two things together.

Un-Du
Manufacturer
888-289-8638 (toll free)
Maker of Un-Du Adhesive Remover and PhotoCare Kits for cleaning photographs.

Xyron
Manufacturer/online catalog
800-793-3523 (toll free)
www.xyron.com
Use Xyron machines for creating stickers, magnets, labels, and laminated materials without heat or electricity; easy for children to use.

Fabrics

Bag Works
Online catalog
3301-C South Cravens Road
Fort Worth, TX 76119
800-365-7423 (toll free)
www.bagworks.com
Canvas bags, aprons, totes, coasters, banners, and more, ready for your photo transfers.

Color Textiles
Manufacturer/online catalog
702-845-5584
www.colortextiles.com
Paper-backed fabrics to facilitate printing; 14 materials available in sheets or rolls. Sample packs available for silks and cottons. Lots of product ideas on the Web site.

Dharma Trading Company
Online and direct-mail catalogs
800-542-5227 (toll free)
www.dharmatrading.com
Silk and cotton fabric sheets prebacked for printing, silk scarves in many sizes, inkjet and copier transfer paper, transfer fabric crayons. Their Web site is a great source of information.

C. Jenkins Necktie Co.
Manufacturer/online catalog
314-521-7544
www.cjenkinscompany.com
Miracle Fabric Sheets (paper-backed white cotton), inkjet printer and copier transfer paper, printable cotton by the yard.

Joann Fabrics and Crafts
Retail stores/online catalog
800-525-4951 (toll free)
www.joann.com
Specializes in fabrics but carries a wide range of craft supplies including scissors and cutting mats, rotary cutters, glues, ribbon, quilt batting and quilt fabrics, color snap tools, foldover binding, Steam-A-Seam fusible web, vinyl and iron-on vinyl, Velcro, unpainted wooden boxes (including tissue boxes).

Silk Connection
Manufacture/online catalog
800-442-0455 (toll free)
www.silkconnection.com
Silk, cotton, and linen fabrics; rayon and silk scarves and ties; white umbrellas.

RibbonShop.com
Online catalog
877-742-5142 (toll free)
www.ribbonshop.com
A great selection of ribbon sold in wholesale quantities.

Paper, Inks, and Canvas

BullDog Products
Manufacturer/online catalog
800-579-8964 (toll free)
www.bulldogproducts.com
Bulldog canvas coated for inkjet printers, spray coating for digital prints on canvas, UltraChrome inks, wide-format paper.

Digital Art Supplies
Online and direct-mail catalogs
877-534-4278 (toll free)
www.digitalartsupplies.com

Great selection of printers, inks, canvas, and paper, including all major brands of fine-art inkjet papers. Also, specialty items such as greeting cards and photo albums. Good source of product information.

Hemmi Papilio
Online catalog
www.papilio.com
817-489-5249
Terrific resource for inkjet and laser specialty films and papers, adhesive-backed paper and film, transfer paper, Water Slide Decal Paper, metallics, magnetic paper, and sealants.

Inkjetart.com
Manufacturer/online catalog
800-777-2076 (toll free)
www.inkjetart.com/www.inkalike.com
InkjetArt Fast-Dry Matte Canvas, plus other supplies for computers and printers including paper, bulk inks, canvas, and slide mounts.

Inkjet Mall
Online catalog
888-426-6323 (toll free)
www.inkjetmall.com
The place for materials for black-and-white printing, archival inks, software, inexpensive inks for Epson printers.

Hiromi Paper International
Retail store/online catalog
2525 Michigan Avenue
Bergamot Sta. G-9
Santa Monica, CA 90404
866-479-2744 (toll free)
www.hiromipaper.com
Very informational site, specializing in a large selection of Japanese papers; printable wood veneer; handmade paper; bookbinding and papermaking supplies; Japanese book cloth.

Hawk Mountain Papers
Online catalog
866-409-4598 (toll free)
www.hawkmtnartpapers.com
High-quality papers coated for inkjet printers; also inkjet canvas and archival inks.

Media Street
Distributor/online catalog
888-633-4295 (toll free)
www.mediastreet.com
Digital supplies, bulk inks, and an excellent selection of artist's papers in hard-to-find sizes.

Micro Format
Online catalog
800-333-0549 (toll free)
www.paper-paper.com,
www.ComputerCrafts.com
Photo-imaging paper and materials, inkjet canvas, specialty papers, parchment and vellum, transfer papers, bumper stickers, labels, adhesive backing for fabric.

Legion Paper
Distributor/limited online catalog
800-278-4478 (toll free)
www.legionpaper.com
Carries over 3,000 papers from around the world; excellent source for high-quality inkjet-printable papers; sells art paper sample packs.

www.paper-paper.com/weight.html
Information
Provides a fabulous conversion table that makes it easy to compare US and metric paper sizes and weights, identifies the different names used for the same weight paper, and supplies a great glossary of paper terms and abbreviations.

Wilhelm Imaging Research
Information
www.wilhelm-research.com
The best resource for current information on ink, printer, and paper-longevity data, conservation information, and permanence testing.

▶ **Furniture and Miscellany**

Home Decorators Collection
Retail stores/online and direct-mail catalogs
8920 Pershall Road
Hazelwood, MO 63042
800-245-2217 (toll free)

www.homedecorators.com
Find folding screens in three styles and several panel options, in black, white, and natural. Also, terrific cabinets that have multiple small drawers to hold all your craft supplies.

Home Depot
Retail stores/online and direct-mail catalogs
800-553-3199 (toll free)
www.homedepot.com
Lots of supplies for photocrafters, like inexpensive unglazed stone tiles.

Unfinished Furniture Showcase
Retail stores/online catalog
228-533-2111
www.unfinishedfurnitureshowcase.com
Unfinished furniture for every room of the house (our source for the wooden plant stand shown on page 134).

▶ **Framing**

ArtFrames
Online catalog
949-646-6555
www.artframes.com
High-quality wood frames at reasonable prices.

PictureFrames.com
Online and direct-mail catalogs
800-221-0262 (toll free)
www.pictureframes.com
Online framing shop with hundreds of choices. You can even upload your image and try it out in any number of mat and frame styles.

Picture Frames 101
Information
www.pictureframes101.com
Not a catalog, but an independent Web site that provides sources for finding framing materials and supplies, plus pros and cons, and how-to information.

 **Special Services**

AAA Flag & Banner Mfg.
Retail stores/online catalog
800-266-4222 (toll free)
www.aaaflag.com
A great place for large-scale and specialty printing needs, including printing on vinyl, nylon, mesh, satin, canvas, polyester, and other unusual materials.

Exposures
Online and direct-mail catalogs
800-222-4947
www.exposuresonline.com
Offers a million ways to frame and present your photographs, including a wide array of albums and frames, plus lockets, bookends, trays, shadow boxes. They will create unique gifts to order from your supplied photos.

NancyScans
Online catalog
800-604-1199 (toll free)
www.nancyscans.com
High-resolution scans at reasonable prices.

photowow.com
Retail store/online and direct-mail catalogs
11950 Wilshire Boulevard
Los Angeles, CA 90025
Store: 310-820-3197
800-453-9333 (toll free)
www.photowow.com
Making large-size canvas prints from your photos is their specialty. Have your photo printed on canvas here or let them also do the image-editing work for you.

CREDITS & ACKNOWLEDGMENTS

The majority of the projects in the book were conceived and created and/or art-directed by Caroline, Laura, and Laurie. Our friends rallied on others by lending ideas, photographs, and fabrication skills—and sometimes all three. We are very grateful for their contributions to the following projects:

Photocraft 101
Frish's Wall
Photographs from the collection of Frish Brandt

Lee's Family Album Quilt
Creator: Lee Sewell

Photo Play
No-Brainer Photo Bracelets
Creator: Stacy Raskin

Slide-Mount Pins
"Molly" photograph © Andrew Hathaway
Beach and island photographs © Katherine Jones

Festive Votives
Creator: Kristie Oaks

Decoupage Suitcase
Creator: Laura Jane Coats
(laurajanecoats@campdeparis.com)
Photographs © Laura Jane Coats, Mary Kashuba, Liz Friend

Kids' Party Invitations
Our party invitation features Ruby Ermine Robinson (ox_bow@hotmail.com).

Holiday Gift Wrap
Photographs © David Graham

Note Cards
Baby feet photograph © Amy Burgess

Your Own Brand
Photographs © Emily Mellor

Mitch's Accordion Frame
Creator: Mitch Nash, cofounder and creative director of Blue Q
Photographs from Mitch's flea market collection
Blue Q makes cool novelty stuff that is sold in book and gift stores nationwide (www.blueQ.com).

Pet Place Mats
Thanks to Sean O'Boyle for lending us Bonnie!

Baby's Bib
Ethel Brennan's adorable no-sew bibs inspired our own. Her book, *Baby Gifts*, is available from Chronicle Books (www.chroniclebooks.com).

Mirror Frame
Concept: Moe Nadel
Photograph © Ed Kashi

Metal Tins
Photographs © Emily Mellor, Katherine Jones

Expanding Your Repertoire
Blueprints
Photographs © Matthew Dula, Sylvie Fourgeot, Doug Logan, Bobbie Osborne, Heather Ringler

Jewel Case Display
Photographs © Jimmy Debruyne, Mark Evans, Benoit Faure, David Graham, Katherine Jones, Laura Lovett, John Rattle, Meredith Tennant, Tomislav Stajduhar

Silk Scarf
Photographs © Mark Tsz Fung, Laura Lovett, Timothy Sullivan

Flea Market Display
Concept: Jeanne Meyers

Growth Chart
Photographs of Eli Kashi © Ed Kashi and Julie Winokur

Throw Pillow
Photograph © Eric Herter

Antique Shoes Baby Quilt
Quilt maker: Susan Melvin

Sylvia's Tote
Creator: Sylvia Holden
Photographs © Sylvia Holden
Sylvia Holden has a 17-year background in fine arts and crafts, having studied at the Fashion Institute of Technology and the Rhode Island School of Design. Her art school training, combined with experience working with antiques at Butterfield & Butterfield Auctioneers, has culminated in high-craft handbags. She mixes love-objects with antique and new materials, creating unique, one-of-a-kind handbags. Her work can be seen at www.sylviaholden.com.

Rearranged Photograph
Creator: Monika Rose
Photograph *"Regenerate"* © Monika Rose

Small Shadow Box
Photograph © Katherine Jones

The Emperor's Box
Creator: Diane Gatterdam
Central photograph © Diane Gatterdam

Accordion-Fold Book
Creator: Lara Hata
Photographs © Lara Hata
Lara Hata is a freelance photographer based in the San Francisco Bay Area. For more information visit her Web site: www.hatamama.com.

Kitchen Clock
Photograph © Katherine Jones
Thanks to Walnut Hollow for the clock makings.

Tile-Topped Plant Stand
Photograph © Paul Elledge

Vellum Lampshades
Creator: Emily Mellor

Carla's Hanging Mural
Creator: Carla Trefethen Saunders
Photographs © Carla Trefethen Saunders
carla@carlatsaunders.com (put project "Photocraft" in the heading—no attachments please)

Folding Screen
Photographs © Joe McDonald
You can view more of Joe's very beautiful work at www.jmcdonaldimages.com.

In addition, we would like to extend our very special thanks to:

Jane Horn, our editor and project writer
An award-winning writer and editor, Jane specializes in food and design. Beyond books, her projects have ranged from catalogs and brochures to online features for national clients like Williams-Sonoma, Dean & DeLuca, and Sunset Books. She holds a Master of Arts in Communication from Stanford University and lives in the San Francisco Bay Area. As a child, she spent many hours as "studio" assistant to her father, a passionate amateur photographer, who she knows would have approved of this book.

Julia Feldman, our craft consultant
Raised in an art and advertising environment, Julia Feldman has never known a time when she wasn't creating art. She received her BFA from California College of Arts & Crafts in 1975 with specialties in Textiles and Metalsmithing. Her continued graduate studies included printmaking, encaustics, and education. More recently Julia has taken her art to digital formats, combining electronic and traditional media in unique ways.

Joseph McDonald, our photography consultant
Joe has been the photographer for The Fine Arts Museums of San Francisco for 15 years and is an Adjunct Professor of Art at Santa Rosa Junior College, where he teaches digital photography. He also has been an exhibiting artist for 25 years, starting with alternative printing processes (primarily platinum printing) and gradually working his way into digital. His photographs are in the collections of The Cantor Arts Center at Stanford University, The Ehrenfeld Collection, Bank of America, and many other public and private collections. As a commercial photographer his clients have included Chronicle Books, Lucasfilm, Pixar Animation Studios, and The Metropolitan Museum of Art.

And to Betty Wong, Karen Murgolo, Jill Cohen, and the fine production and copyediting department at Bulfinch Press: Thank you for your support and expert guidance throughout.

—CH, LF, LL

Photocraft was conceived and produced for Bulfinch Press by
HERTER STUDIO LLC
(www.herterstudio.com)

INDEX